Dead Cat Bounce

Dead Cat Bounce

New and Selected Poems

John Carey

PUNCHER & WATTMANN

First published in 2021
Published by Puncher & Wattmann
PO Box 279
Waratah NSW 2298

puncherandwattmann@bigpond.com

NATIONAL
LIBRARY
OF AUSTRALIA

A catalogue entry for this book is available from the National Library of Australia.

ISBN   9780925780949

Cover design by Miranda Douglas

Printed by Lightning Source International

This project has been assisted by the Australian Government through the Australia Council, its arts funding and advisory body.

Australian Government

Australia
Council
for the Arts

Contents

from *One Lip Smacking*

from *Duck Soup and Swansongs*

Recent Poems

Early Poems 1968-75

A Beggar in May

The dream began with pizza:
bulging black olives, bristling anchovies,
scattered on the fuming tripes of a volcano.
Fuelled with red wine he flew
to a silken rape in a confusion
of perfumed sheets. His head filled
with little gold lights of mimosa pudica
and the villa echoed with educated sighs
till his wings iced over and dawn mist
licked his misery into shape.
A very clean-cut Samurai
leapt from an election poster,
kneed him in the groin and asked
for an interview. Tonight he will dream
the avenger dream, a death list, letters
to the heavier-breathing sector
of the press, threats very much to the point.
Still yoked with the habit of a park bench,
he fights for balance in air ablaze
with church bells.

(Marseille 1968)

Céline

In prose that sputtered
like a smutty candle,
under his pen a mishap
swelled to a disaster
and when things couldn't be worse,
they got worse.
His books dancing to a paranoiac's crooked
tune corkscrewed into
hell or
silence.

> Up the dead-end street
> Of the Choiseul Passage
> they were heartsick with greed
> and disappointment. Doctor Destouches
> fell in love with the diseases
> and drowned in his own bile,
> no Jew-baiting monster, just a man
> with monstrously bad taste
> and the arrogance of a good pro,
> the Jack Johnson of the pen-men.

There were a lot of things Ferdinand
never asked.
He never asked to be born.
He was dropped free-fall into the smoky
twilight of a losers' world
and never stopped wanting
to go back. He is still
falling.

Small Town Sketches

I
I wake in a bed
my body has not yet learned
and find myself a six-thousandth
of the known world.
Already I am reminded of nothing.
Two pubs, a club, a dip in the baths,
a feed at the Chows and the town
will be in the bag and me with it.
I will wear a name and function
like a hump on my back.

II
I am lying in dry grass
by the tea-coloured river.
There is a short-circuit in my head.
Wires are crackling there like cicadas.
A train goes past on the branch line
over the bridge maybe twice a week.
I feel like I have fallen off
once on the way to somewhere.

III
We are all legends in our own time.
The most unmysterious deaths are noticed.
Soon I will pick up my skin at the station
cloakroom, try it for size and ride
into the vast cemetery of Elsewhere,
one of the people who did one of the things

that happened last year when you should
have been there.

IV
Tom is a dairy-farmer
with knobby hands that do his thinking
for him. Something I let slip
made him sure I meant
to socialise him, collectivise him,
force his daughter to commit unnatural acts,
take his livestock, his land
and his brass and generally
bugger him. He gives me a lesson in politics
with a jarring handshake.

V
They like jokes where the loser
chops the big man down.
"So I says: Gasnier, you're not
worth a pinch of shit"
was the sort of punchline
and their eyes say: laugh on cue
or take your turn in the barrel.

VI
There is a short list of known criminals
who know they are known and are known
to know they are known.
They nick things with a modus operandi
predictable as a spider web.
They stay because they are not ambitious
and feel they are more or less wanted.

VII
A nickname is as near to character analysis
as decency will permit.
Mine is "Jesus"— my initials have something
to do with it, plus in my cups
I am sure they are out to get me
and tell them so, a blatant provocation.
I creep, they say,
always wearing brothel-creepers
and walking on the balls of my feet.
There will be worse to come.

Cave

In the abattoir queue
fear ripples down the line
with a hoarse, keening whisper.
Small birds struggle in the net of my skin.
My saliva is foul with terror.
Cacus at the entrance
in one monstrous inhalation
has swallowed all the light and air
in the world.

We keep kinetic time
in our cavernous sleep
rolling   tale over teller over told
spokes of the same wheel.

from *Sorting through Wardrobes*
(Ginninderra Press 2004)

Web Site

In the nineteen-fifties, a scientist employed by Naval Intelligence
or some other oxymoronic wing of the Pentagon,
blew a five million dollar allocation
on tests that involved blowing marijuana smoke
non-stop into a nest of spiders to check the effect
on their web-weaving, fly-swaddling
and other spiderly domestic chores.
Sure enough, the webs grew ragged and flaccid
and the flies began to buzz teasingly close,
making a mockery of the air defences
and dropping their eggs in the spiders' whiskers.
The dope-crazed arachnids forsook all ambition,
embraced promiscuity, not a pretty sight,
and gave up all attempts at personal hygiene.
There were outbreaks of schizophrenia,
the legs of the stricken dialectically ordered
in groups of four, pulling in different directions.
Some took to wearing berets and corduroy jackets,
scatting be-bop and climbing the walls at Birdland.
Others hitched rides on fruit trucks
heading back to California
and howled Whitmanesque sonnets
at the windswept prairies.

Annapolis' answer to Pavlov
must have sucked when he was meant to blow
the day he announced stage two of the project:
to inject funnel-webs with heroin
and measure reaction times and fine motor skills
on a series of routine tasks, like mothball juggling,
pleading the fifth and riding a unicycle.
I never saw a report of his findings.

I can only assume he underestimated
his subjects' first-strike capability.

A Film by Eric Rohmer

You notice subliminally what's not there:
no crags, chasms, riots of colour, trackless
wastes of land, sea or sky, nothing to shrink us.
There are no grand architectural follies
or monuments to shove history in our faces.
These are landscapes tamed and smoothed by the passage
of a billion holidays — the lake at Annecy,
the beach at Dinard — that make no statements
to drown us out, lands of the internal tourist,
no black faces, no whiff of the Mahgreb,
a uniculture with a stud book
unsullied by mixed marriages, reaching back
to Marivaux and Madame de Sévigné.
Even the interiors whisper discreetly:
un petit café, un petit cognac,
un petit air de guitare, un petit bouquin,
un petit projet de voyages—drugs and dreams
in miniature. There are no boys and girls
from the rumbling belly of the slums,
no interfering parents, no traumas
in backpacks to be dragged out, ripped and spilled.
It is a world of singles and siblings,
a secular Church Fellowship, where pairing off
depends on an interface of yearnings,
a happy conjuncture of time and place,
a well dropped confession or non-confession.

I wonder why the films travel so badly?
An absence of kung fu, car-trashing, casual smut
that empties cinemas worldwide? Cultural static?
We are a long way here from schoolies week at Surfers,
even further from bingeing on Schlitz and tits
at Biloxi. We stamp our feet at the stasis

of young people who talk and talk,
before, instead of and never afterwards,
for and about themselves, into timid first steps
and bold projects, then out of them again,
moved by aesthetic imperatives and a moral
primness that we like to pretend makes no sense.
And yet. Airbrush out the larrikin smudges
from our own lives and imagine an adolescence
where we finished sentences, said what we meant
in our own voices, and there is a shaming
similarity. We remember most the waiting —
for a fiancée to come back, for a platonic
friend to betray herself with a trembling lip,
for the adult world to pin us to the ground
and talk us stupid. We remember the grim truth
that sex never solved anything unless it failed,
miserably and often, how a girl was forced
to steer a course between whore and Virgin Mary
in patient head-spinning negotiation;
how boys never stopped counting— the plus and minus
of being more assertive, the endless steps
to total power or total self-control.

I stroll in the celluloid oasis with my wife,
far from the sandstorms of social determinism
and afterwards we discuss what we each saw
from the perspective of our own particular planet.
At night I imagine other lives, other lovers,
rustling through the pages of our dreams,
sorting through wardrobes for clothes and grown-up shoes
to totter towards us, grinning, in the morning.

A Recipe for Nausea

A book doesn't squat in a space
like a Magritte print on the wall
in a sight line you can manipulate
within certain limits only
as you wrap your senses round
an anecdote without a punchline
and find it arbitrary but firmly itself.
Every book I halfway like
squirms as it tries to match itself
to a Cinderella's slipper in my cortex.
A book becomes a slice of the reader's life
measured in journeys, plateaux
on an affective graph or a chart
of therapies for conditions
as yet undiagnosed.

An author who is loved for a misunderstanding
is usually grateful for it, accepting this
as better than the opposite case,
though I suspect that Jean-Paul Sartre
would have cowed me with his wall-eyed stare
if I'd confessed that I understood
next to nothing of his major work
but managed to move myself to tears
with a few pages of La Nausée.
I warmed to the idea of common objects
stickily resistant under torture
that refused to give up names
and serial numbers to a bookworm,
at a lacuna in his life, engaged

in shadowy research in a medium-sized
provincial city of little charm.

I permitted myself an easy familiarity
as I took the protagonist by the arm
and guided him to a library
on the Place de l'Hôtel de Ville.
We watched as an assistant
snatched a quick look at a paper
requesting access to a forgotten monograph,
then disappeared down corridors
into more and more restricted areas,
shutting doors behind her.

I had by now moved into my own book
where I turned the page and watched her come back,
saying yes to the piece of paper,
and yes, she had a blank weekend in front of her
and needed to fall into a pit of arms, legs
and seething propositions that tasted like cruelty.
Innocent of any philosophy,
I rewrote the book as a study in loneliness,
on a train once,
young it must have been,
on the cusp of something
moving into something else.

The Poetics of Surfing

At the Scott's Head colloquy of 1969,
proceedings began with the lighting,
by the Californians, of a ceremonial bong
with a crater like a Mexican volcano.
The first American to the rostrum
was Quentin Brown the Third, renunciate heir
to a real estate empire, who spoke prayerfully
of merging with the surge of creation
and defined the perfect wave
as the mighty utterance of the great 'Om!'

Waster Watson, the local champion,
rose to rebut and said that, for him,
the Pacific was the start of something
not the finish, and he was going to take those sets
by the scruff of the neck and give them a caning.

And they argued on till plover-screech,
finally agreeing to two propositions:
You can't put an old Restoration hairdo
on young shoulders
and the grass is always cleaner and cheaper
from a little farm near Mullumbimby.

Rupert Drops in to the Office

A prat-scan uncovers a nest of them,
of Identikit vagueness, alike as two peas
in a whistle, in a Green Room backstage
of a One-Man-Show that never closes.
They are going down on mobile phones
in a drool of erectile expectations.
A wisp of headline rhetoric spirals into the air
like smoke from a gun as they orbit
the guru, rearrange his limbs,
pick burrs from his hair, decode
his glossolalia and offer him kidneys
and virgin daughters. They assure him
that he has a praetorian guard so hard-bitten
they have bitten off their own ethics
to free themselves from a poverty trap.
The ex-editorialist of the Guardian
is swearing on a stack of share options
that when he once spoke of 'a rotting
harvester of hard currency' he was referring
to the corpse of Lenin
not his new master.

The Laurieton Plaza

Where the strip shops cut out, on the corner
of the turn to the Fishermen's Co-Op,
before the High Street slopes off
down to the South bridge,
is the only boutique cinema
in the land of Rural and Regional—
plush red seats, gilt-trimmed proscenium,
a foyer at the charming end of kitsch.
The old barn with the thundering tin roof
has been stripped and refashioned
into the stumbled-upon discovery
the tourist brochure never thinks to mention.
We see a film we wouldn't normally choose,
a flimsy feel-good where likeable young people
get their just deserts plus twenty per cent.
We have coffee on the landing
by the blue trellis screens.
The olive-green loom of North Brother Mountain
flicks a last clinging hang glider
off into the humming twilight.
A pygmy bat robs moths from a street lamp.
The Summer Holiday starts to peel itself back
to a bare archetype long forgotten –
a smell of salt and frangipani,
midges dancing on the yellow face of the moon
and the night murmuring strategies
you have no names for.

Changing Patterns in the Avifauna of Sydney

big birds
big no-nonsense birds
big look-you-in-the-eye larrikin birds
even the little ones pushy
and tough like jockeys
and loud loud birds
that straddle your brain at first light
and pick it clean
whingeing and sledging
no muted pastel birds no shy indeterminates
these are the birds of events
and gushing fireworks
birds we earned
birds we deserve
top-of-the-podium birds
I'll-take-the-fuckin'-packet birds
winners

Letter to my Cousin

At University, I could see only your freckled awkwardness
and the clichéd images of my own teenage omniscience:
I thought you asexual, so far from sensuality and comeliness
that nobody could want you but an Irish God,
in the image and likeness of a parish priest who measured out
his hedonism, drip by drip, in hot-water bottles and whisky.
I watched you negotiate your way through the neo-pagan
cloisters and sceptical lectures into the fullest profession
of your Faith. If we ever spoke, we stayed in the safest
conversational zones—no more than politeness
on my part; for you, already, something deeper and richer,
respect perhaps or charity? When I saw you at Christmas,
I understood that in your daily commerce with the poor
and desperate, you had seen more of life than I had.
When I asked you how you coped, your smile was fuller
and franker than I remembered it. "You have to keep
in mind that you're not the judge" you said,
"more like the prisoner's friend."

Past middle-life, when most of us ease back on it a little,
you studied Spanish in Bolivia, went to Chile and Peru
to set up 'Women's Houses' in the slums, giving lessons
in work skills and human dignity. Your mother showed me photos
of you, standing by a grey concrete bunker
that perched on a wilderness of toxic landfill,
shepherding your stunted garden into growth,
and beside you, Indian women, in candy-striped shorts
and baseball-caps, smiling through broken teeth
in the orange dust of the barrio, with their newborn pride
pushing the shyness aside. I imagine you putting
your humble certainties in the way of brilliantined ponces
with knives strapped to their calves and husbands
crazed with pisco and bruised machismo, or haggling

with the tanker-men who bring the daily ration of water,
talking them into swapping their petty extortion
and the Sunday pitcher of beer it brings them
for a dry portion of righteous self-esteem.

I repent of the black jokes about flying nuns
pitched out of helicopters, in a latter-day witch test,
by CIA agents with names like Jablonski or O'Malley.
What joke could I make about another missionary Sister,
your colleague and friend, made to kneel, and shot
in the back of the head, for daring to outshine
the Shining Path? Or her refusal to add one more splash
of anger to the torrent, preferring to call down God's blessing
on the mental and moral defectives who rushed her
into His Presence? Was there some chivalrous Prince
of the Church, ready to come by chauffeured limousine
from Lima to take her place?
"If God had willed it" you say. Yes.

Pussy Whipped

The cat pads to the bedroom, trailing a muffled
cry, to tell me that the sun that filled the defile

between curtain and glass-door has been cloud-snuffed
and demands that the matter be set to rights

or a half-hour of bed rest on the living
warmth of my stomach. Won over by her faith

in my powers and condescension, I give in,
doling out caresses for compensation

and am pinned to the bed by sloth and devotion,
out of reach of pen and palimpsest.

I call to mind a tip for aspiring poets:
'Whatever else you do each day, get dressed!'

From *The Old Humanists*
(Puncher & Wattmann 2008)

The Armagh School of Positivism

For the last ten years of his life
Father O'Meara gave the same sermon,
whatever the text he started from,
with the same key phrases:
"very, very definitely
and very, very positively"
like drum-rolls before a last restatement
of the opening theme.

In synopsis, it went like this:
the word of God is the Word of God
not the word of Franklin or Jefferson
that needs a panel of judges sitting in permanence
to pick over it. The Universe
is not a rebus to be solved
but logical perfection imperceptible only
to the proud and the wilfully stupid
and if there is any attempt
to blast exegesis out of its well-oiled grooves
then it is the hand of Lucifer
pressing the plunger.
As a corollary, it was clear
that whoever associated the Society of Jesus
with casuistry would have to answer to him
and it certainly wasn't an Irishman,
not even a Presbyterian, to give them their due,
however blind they were in their Error.

When he was old and failing,
the starting text and its development
started to slip away
to the point where "very, very definitely
and very, very positively"

were the only form and content
like a question that went on answering itself
for what seemed like eternity.

Already a fledgling agnostic
and timid hedonist who would rather
be anywhere else than in church,
I had a mean thought:

"I'd like to see the look on his face
when there is no look on his face
when he sees what happens
when nothing happens."
He had taught me no theology
but had made me an honours student
of Irish logic.

Later, when my own certainties
had bruised and softened,
I thought of him, out of the pulpit,
as a wise confessor and a kind man.
The God of no-paradoxes and no-surrender
had made a sort of paradox
of this, his creature.
And most of the others. Most of us.

New Fiction: 1965

This the soundtrack of the movie
adaptation of a story I never wrote.
There are footfalls on the cobblestones
of a dockside street in Northern Europe
unevenly spaced in trochee and anapaest
suggesting the clump of an unsound
or prosthetic limb. You hear the sizzle
of a faulty neon sign in an unfashionable
language, upside down in reflection
from an unspecified liquid surface.
An accordion, certainly, hornpipe
or harmonica not out of the question.
There is a hawker's cry in some synthetic
dialect you recognise immediately
as pure hawker. Then a woman's
high heels clattering on the pavement
like a mitraillette and small wheels
jinking over an uneven surface –
a baby-carriage? Can pavement
co-exist with cobblestones? Who would
walk the baby in high heels? We have
an ambience, an enigma, a hint
of disablement, the promise
of a transaction. Time to pause
to let the story breathe and consider
its next move. Each side alley leads
into a genre where gangs of readers,
territorial as tomcats, wait in ambush.
I let it breathe some more, the sound
of the story breathing magnified as if
amplifiers are sunk into its very soul.
Then silence. The decision is not mine.

Each story chooses its own demise
and the manner in which it goes.

Unmaking the Inventory

The books - thousands of lives, invented mostly
encrypted in an old technology
with no heirs you can think of
likely to visit the graves.

A clay statuette of an Aztec fire god
mass produced and uncommunicative
like the love affair it was a relic from.

Art works by my wife's father and sister.
How can you separate with any sureness of touch
reverence for the personal histories
and reverence for the paintings?

A print from the Peggy Guggenheim Collection.
Venice in Autumn sunshine - I am thinking
of the acquisition, not the print - the lagoon pristine
from a distance, the canals a benign milky-green,
safely short of overlapping and spoiling
the texture of a second honeymoon.

A print from the Musée Marmottan:
The docks of Le Havre at dawn. Monet's
signature in large white script
drawing the light to itself.

A television, CD player and speakers
which sit hugely in their space
but when switched off are somehow
invisible, as if the sounds and stories

that live there are wintering
in a better climate.

A lounge-suite which has lasted
as long as our marriage, longer than most.
Lounge-suites. And marriages.
The old cat who was young once
has gouged pieces out of the arm rests
with the claws we were too busy to clip.

And the dresser, older still, bought in a market
more raffish then, less twee, where the bargains fell
off the back of a better class of truck. The maker and I
are roughly equidistant from the point of sale -
seven decades of separation.

As it grows dark, the stories are muffled.
Assessment takes on the quantifiable
certainty of bulk and brute geometry.
It is all loom and heft, shinbark
and knucklescrape. The print acquired
in Venice: Magritte's "L'Empire
des Lumières" has switched off
its last unlikely streetlamp
and doused its impossible sunlight.

Update

(after "This Be the Verse" by Philip Larkin)

They prop you up, your mum and dad
and cushion you against the blows
who'll never have the chance they had
to shun the grindstone, keep their nose

in storybooks till old enough
to love their life above their station
and seek the truth behind the puff
of salesmen for a lean, mean nation.

They're sad because they couldn't bear
to see you sour and robbed of hope
and shamed because you're all aware
that in your shoes, they couldn't cope.

Migration of a line from W.G. Sebald

In her sister's portrait, my wife at seventeen –
more than a decade before I knew her –
looks over Shoal Bay from Fort Tomaree
in profile but half turned away,
the line of her jaw and point of her chin
at once unknown and familiar, her thick hair
tied at the back with a yellow ribbon,
and seems to follow the curving flight
of a seagull, caught between rising sea mist
and the evanescent streaming of clouds.

As I stare at it in the uncertain light
of a reading-lamp meeting the first rays
of the sun, the painting seems to tremble
and flip to the next frame, like a new
month of a calendar or the last tumble
of a stopped sequence of animation.
She has turned, sensing her sister's diffidence
at painting her full-face (though this
was years later, from a photograph)
and her half-smile seems to say:
"why should we be afraid, either of us?"
as if she knew in this one gesture
that she had the gift of being remembered.

Bringing the People Back

From the outside, the old wool-store
has kept its close-mouthed integrity.
But inside it has been gutted, stuffed
with low-maintenance greenery and sliced
into Security Prestige Apartments, so the residents
can turn their backs on the teeming streets
and gaze at each other's navels. The visitor
needs a voiceprint in triplicate to get to the desk
to give the password to get the key for the
moat and portcullis giving access to Parking
and another for the axle-cracker that guards each space.

In case you run off with the keys and admit
the entire population of Cabramatta one night
for a parking lot knees-up, you leave a deposit:
driver's licence, credit cards, fistfuls of foreign
currency, deeds to your home and a promissory
note for your daughter's virginity. When I saw
the artificial leg nailed to the concierge's desk,
I asked the girl: "Miracle Cure?"
"Key defaulter" she said, "he won't get far."

Urban High-Rise

The roof pool hawks and spills.
Through the glass, a crane sprouts
from a hillock of rubble.
A woman puts a shivering
Maltese terrier into a carry bag
then tests each machine in the gym
thoughtfully. In the street, a jogger tosses
a mobile phone from hand to hand,
muttering: "she loves me, she loves me not."
Security have spotted an unexplained
child skipping and are dealing with it
without fuss. The keepers of Convenience
Village update the Community
Notice-Board on page three
of the Website and wait for the goods
to walk out the door, leaving a tip.
The block opposite flashes
a harmonica-grin, the lit teeth
running chromatics as you enter the lift.
It finds your keycard enigmatic and stalls.
You let it read the barcode on your jacket
that spells out an evening agenda
of scented spa and self-pleasuring
and it relaxes into a soundless descent.
You are experiencing the lifestyle,
bought off the plan. The lift-doors let you out
directly into the hallway of an apartment
quite like the one you left this morning.
You will search the Net for a decorator
steeped in the concept of Sprawl
to guide you into making this your own.

Prohibitions on Tour

In the Adelaide Art Gallery: "No Helium Balloons"
in a pub at Glenelg (and others): "No Exposed Tattoos"
in Wagga Mall: "No Wheeled Recreational Devices"
in a spa at Blackheath: "Appropriate Behaviour Expected
at All Times". In the Commercial Club at Albury:
"No Tight Jeans". And an overseas entry
from the intimidating elevation of the Pont du Gard:
"Défense de Plonger!"

And you wonder. And wish you'd seen what happened
to make them put up the sign: the Art-thieves floating
a heroic Fragonard up to a waiting helicopter,
the Tahitian breasts and Maori buttocks
and the marine non-com whose limp "W O" expanded
to "WOOLLOOMOOLOO" at full stretch,
the souped-up golf-buggies and V-8
trolleys, the Blue Mountains Swingers' Club
performing a full version of "The Aristocrats",
Border bouncers touch-testing the tautness
of trousers, the New Zealand bungee-jumpers
catching mullet with their teeth.

Is it all a tease, inviting you to stock your brain
with samples for an Imaginary Museum
like a sign I once saw in a cantina
in Franco's Spain: "Se Prohibe Cantar!"
to let you know that behind the austere facade,
the power-cuts, the tortured plumbing,
the preventive detentions and provocateurs,
was a song in full bud ready to burst into flower.

Speech from the North Coast Business Awards

I set up the Twilight Home for Alternative Lifestylers
on an old yabby-farm 10 K from Kyogle
as a tax-offset, sure, but also an act of piety —
a place where Mum and Dad could play their Eric Bogle
tapes, put their moccasins up and wrap their gums
round a few quiet bongs at the end of the day.
I was, after all, the battle they never won,
seduced by the real Estate scramble at Byron Bay.

Soon old friends joined them, one by one,
two by two, sometimes three by three, jetsam
of communes, of the war against substances
that threatened public order and public hysteria,
guitar-stringers, candle-makers, growers of clean vegetables
whose wastrel sons and daughters had fled to the city
to work in Marketing, smoke their inheritance
and mate with the clean-shaven and the blandly pretty.

I see this as the first of a misty Archipelago
of Last Resorts that will suck service-jobs
back out of the city to places like Dorrigo,
the Tweed hinterland, even Barrington Tops.
These will be the Indian reservations of New South Wales
with guided tours to suit the tourist's needs —
Casinos where the wheel spins slowly, sales
of psychedelic ponchos and venerable beads.

Memoirs of a Little Rodent

When the policemen were older
the postmen had whistles
and the Queen was a slip of a girl
when the South Pole was colder
and Ming had his Thistle
and Mum wore a twinset and pearls
when the menace was red
and the peril was yellow
and the pollies all sucked up to Ike
then you did what Dad said
liked your music mellow
and you had to earn your first bike.

Who'd ever have thought
fifty years down the track
that I'd settle at Kirribilli
in a house I never bought
with views front and back
as the President's favourite gillie?
I uphold the rule of Laws
I cannot tell a lie
I've chopped down no cherry-tree
like Louis Quatorze
I resolve not to die
till the State is the image of me.

Grey Nomads

When the last dog died (this would be the last
they swore), there was no more reason to walk
these too-familiar streets in all weathers.
They sold the house, inherited once too often,
with the spreading empty spaces and the junk-mail
telling them who and what they were:
householders, consumers, tickers of the last box:
their own kids with their customised partners
and the grandkids, time-managed till they disappeared
into their own schedules. "We'll miss you!"
they said, as the baby-sitters waved goodbye.

They are in the here and now and gone tomorrow.
Let the city consolidate itself in the space they left
and they won't give a bugger as they suck
mudcrab-claws in the van park at Keppel Sands
with a couple of coldies and a sing-song
of Golden Oldies. This is the life they owe themselves
after watching Nan mummified in her TV shrine
and Pop in his lost worlds of bricolage
in the shed at the back. They have made old bones
and will set them clicking to a different tune –
a bag-lady and a homeless gent
in a roaring handcart half a block long.

They pass the months touring Shearers' Museums
on cattle and mission stations, ways of life
they knew before only as shadows cast by monuments
or disappearing down back lanes.
They make new friends – a lesbian couple
they would never have wanted as neighbours,
an old doctor and his dress-designer wife
from a suburb where their own tribe never ventured

except to empty garbage and mow lawns.
They are covering their tracks with bland postcards
as they make their own road movie in their heads
with a free and easy focus and chronology.

Fathers Day in Broome —" a scene of confusion"
says their mischievous guide. The locusts on the Nullabor
turning the windshield into a sepia frame with streaks
and runnels like cough syrup gathering
in the corners. And the frames where the story
stalls in freshets of unnameable colour — Spring plains
after rain in the Pilbara, storm hatching
in Kimberly skies before the first monsoon,
the touch of zebra-rock, seed-pearl and wet jasper.
At Christmas, back in Sydney for the usual pieties,
they seem to be visiting their own graves
with armfuls of wildflowers to say adieu.

Coup de Théâtre

The speaker for our orientation address
was a theatre director, known to turn
princes and princesses of arts journalism
into frogs before his snake-like stare.
He stood and glared at us for three minutes
till a few whistles and slow handclaps
rippled round the auditorium.
"That's better" he said "If you tolerate tedium
you're sure to inflict it." Then he began
with a story of a story that went like this:

"I had another class of putative actors once
and I showed them stills from a film –
a series of close-ups of a young oriental woman
whose face ran through a gamut of emotions
and I asked them to supply a narrative
to match the pictures. They served up plots
from grand opera and soap opera, plus
some more condensed lyricism of the sort:
'she is looking through the windows of a passing train
for the face of a long-lost lover.' One wag
gave himself away by suggesting
that she had trained her cat to walk up and down
all over her body, treading corn.
Then I told them the truth: someone had filmed
a political prisoner in China in the nineteen thirties
being slowly tortured to death."

He went on to talk about the Strasberg Heresy —
how emotions truthfully felt and expressed
were no guarantee of communication
and a corollary: how the language of theatre
often travelled badly through space and time.

I found myself choking on a subtext
that had nothing to do with contending schools of theatre.
If a snuff movie existed, he was ready to use it
for the sake of art or pedagogy. If not,
he would invent it and let a frisson loose
to slither through a first-night audience
or chill the earnest hearts of a drama class
on a smug provincial campus.

I didn't believe his story
and he could have made the same point by telling us
that she was threading difficult shoelaces
into a new pair of Reeboks.

Fidel's Children

The mechanic who can kick the mutest junkpile back to life
and swear fluently in three Slavonic languages.
The Minister of Finance who remembers fondly
burning off the leeches of the Sierra Maestra with a Zippo.
A seminarian who quotes Lenin and on weekends
has been known to do disgusting things with a chicken.
The ancient coal-black hotel porter, grandson
of a slave, who at the age of eighty-five,
can lug forty kilos of baggage three floors
up a spiral staircase and boasts how he learned to read
under the Five Week Plan of 1960.
The Mambo Queen who once sang torch songs
for Lucky Luciano, working on a new ballad
that says in rough translation: "Sure,
there are fuck-ups but they're our fuck-ups!"
The veteran Colonel of the Angolan campaign
turned tourist entrepreneur, doing so well
she sends money to help cousins in Miami.

The village of protected witnesses

is one of an archipelago of gated estates
based on the model of a neighbourhood of Phoenix
acquired by the FBI in the nineteen-eighties.
People pull coats up over their heads to collect the mail.
The Infants' School has its own Hearing Clinic
for children who fail to answer to their names.
Everyone goes to the same barber for the same haircut
and the same cosmetic surgeon for the same nose.

The atmosphere is benign, as it should be.
Being in a certain place at a certain time
is not in itself a crime, though refusal
to cooperate takes on a darker colour
that will earn for some a single ticket
to the Village of Rendered Prisoners
where they learn Information Technology
from the angle of the cutting edge
and escape only through the loading-bay
of the Rendering Plant. Democracy thrives
in this, the village of the undamned
within the parameters laid down
by the manager "Call-me-Rodney",
late of the North West Mounted Police.

Short-term residents, whose cases are brought
swiftly to trial, seldom want to return
but those on standby for seven years or more
are allowed back (vetted and blindfolded)
to give the village a stratum of leadership
and act as counsellors for those new arrivals
still bereft of their old, untidy lives.

The Heretic Insists

(for Christine)

The heretic insists. It isn't this I cherish:
the Risen Christ, the theist's thin tenets,
their incense, their ethics — in essence
reins, cinches, ice-teeth in the ether.

It's esthetic, isn't it? — nine senses erect,
the intense secrets in their centre,
their hinter, their nether. It's ciné-tints
in the streets — cerise, citrine.
It's the chic, the recherché, rich
scents in heiresses' sheets.

It's the crescent itch,
the thirst in Circe's shrine,
the tenseness in the testes,
the thresh in the seine-nets,
their seethe, their hiss.
It's in thee, chérie, entire.

These irises shine.
This isn't tristesse.
It's Ceres serene.

Madonna: the Paris Concert

```
                        E        D
                  M                        U
            A
                                              S

   L                                                  E

   a                                                    l
   m     l         a     l     e     l     a     l
   e     l         m     u     e     u     l     e
   s     u         e     e     s     l     u
         m     l               s     e     e     s
   d     e         l     d     e                       e
   e     u         e     e           a     l     u
         s         s                 d           a     l
   s     e                     l     u     l'          e
   e               m     a               au-   m
   l     m         a                 M     d     a     e
         a         s     M     a     e     s     l
         l         s     u     l     l     s     l
         a         e         s             a     e     e
         d         e         e
         e         s                                        s
                                                            e
                                                            u
                                                            l
                                                            e
```

Brains on the Table

As matter, off-white rather than grey,
a couple of fistfuls of blubbery heft,
they can be carried in a knotted handkerchief,
will fit a medium-sized casserole or bain-marie,
can be cooked in a pint of court-bouillon,
served with black butter or in any of a dozen
preparations; if you can't make up your mind,
check Larousse Gastronomique under "offal".

In the wards and theatres,
they deal with the brain as a cunning
governor of pumps and bellows, clutch
and apprehension, intelligible only
as non-trauma, un-bruise, what functions
when all the diverticula are sluiced,
defined by distance from madness,
shell-shock and trepannage. When
the brain, made whole, starts to explain
itself to itself, their job is done.
They call in the metaphysicians.

Or the theologians who posit a tracking
device, implanted by persons unknowable,
He, She, or They having nothing better to do
than play hide-and-seek with their own
better Nature. When each epiphany pulses
forth from the launch-pad, a million
synapses clamber over one another
to shout Hosanna. Theirs is the Good News.
For pain management, it's back to the quacks

for dosing and tinkering or with luck
a craftily guided chemical pillow.

But the real interest, we are told,
is in the product, not the factory:
the mind as distinct from ideas,
reasoning, creativity. How do I plan
a backpack tour of this area in a few
snapshots? Given that I hear the earth
crack and see an abyss yawning
when a French acquaintance explains
that she is holidaying in Martinique
this year, instead of Morocco
"pour changer les idées"
or whenever a lover tells me:
"I've changed my mind."

The Suspect

His smug self-possession was highly suspicious.
His eagerness to help set the bells ringing.
His growing alarm was inconsistent with innocence.
His bewilderment was a piece of crafty staging.
His stoicism suggested a long apprenticeship.
His disclosures of guilt were carefully managed:
once bullying a younger brother, an unpaid loan,
thoughts of adultery he took some pleasure in—
a smokescreen of personal shame
to hide what we really wanted to know.
His relief when we promised to release him
settled the issue. To sum it up,
he behaved like a man who has been arrested
and we're not the sort to arrest a man for nothing.

Motivation

At the counselling session, the leader makes it clear
that this isn't the village general store
where selling is an exchange of rich civilities
but more like bass fishing with a minimum
bag-limit, when the bass must be convinced
that they are hungry. Suspecting that I may
be tainted with altruism, he tells me to keep in mind
the future school fees of my future children
and the dream home my future wife will surely expect.
At some point, my traitorous eyebrows give me away.
Mitch's face takes on the jowled menace
of a De Niro character holding a skittish
informant by the ankles as he hangs
from the window of the thirtieth floor.
"Of course," he says, "we may have to let you go."

Conspiracy

You don't know your onions but they are round like plums
so you strip an onion, looking for a hard core.
Nothing. It looks undisturbed but someone has been here before,
smashed the seed to sub-atoms with a particle-gun
or excised it with a laser-knife and stitched it all back, invisibly.
You and the onion are the victims of Conspiracy.

In a dream you are the tiniest Russian doll
given rat-teeth by a Secret Angel in the service of Light.
You gnaw your way out through each sibling's splintered vitals
into the fetid air of a sealed coffin.
The world as Necropolis? A kind of grim symmetry...
You are learning the Kabbala of Conspiracy.

You choose a lover who drags like a spavined mare
into each unpromising dawn, her eyes the stains
of the sinned-against, her arms a collaboration.
You are her soldier-saviour of the thousand-yard stare.
Your two hearts beat as two but with a quiet complicity.
Fear of its double is all that troubles Conspiracy.

You have tracked and deciphered till it all converges
into the One Cause, the single rotten cell
that makes all life a death-sentence. Your brain swells
into a bursting choir-loft as the Voices name the murderers
of Princes, loved ones, children. They are a Satanic Trinity,
three whispers into a single breath: Conspiracy.

The Shed at the Back Revisited

everything is as it seems   shaped like its shape
the tools were used to build the tool-rack
the sawdust comes in bags   that's the gardener's job
and spread near the drinks-cabinet   retro estaminet
there's heating but in the winter months I prefer
to mutilate the soft toys in my bedroom
the collection was widely scattered and will be again
sadistic plushophilia   there's a website
teddy/Iwon'twarnyouagain.com
I'm locking up now   you can put your shoes back on
but keep whispering   I think I have a headache

I needed to find myself

picking up the trail at one of those points
where I might have strayed – the junction
of the first, second and third persons,
a pivotal moment like the birth of a first child
when one watches oneself close one's eyes
for not knowing where to look. Or when love
first made itself known without equivocation
shining in the only pair of eyes
you would ever want to see yourself through.
Or was it more recently, in the memory zone
grown pallid with indifference, when I stopped
observing for fear I would understand too well?
Perhaps I doubled back. I look back along the track
to see the grass beaten flat. In one direction only.

From *One Lip Smacking*
(Picaro Press 2013)

Sam Spade's Monday

My sock-drawer is hosting a Singles Party.
My old slippers have hidden the new ones.
My clothes feel cold and slip me on under them.
The month's free trial of my hair-piece
ends tomorrow. My line of credit
at the liquor-store has gone dead.
The bank is holding my money for ransom.
The car I tried to have boosted for the
insurance wouldn't start. My only call
is a phone survey on business confidence.
The broad I tried to save went back to her pimp.
The kids have given me weekend custody
of my ex-wife and her mother.

The lock on my office has given up.
Sitting in my chair, feet up on my desk,
her scarlet toenails tickling my diploma,
her long legs heading for trouble,
is a woman I have never seen before
except in one of those dreams
you wouldn't even tell your shrink.
She gives me a Mona Lisa smile and purrs:
"Mr. Rosendahl, I'm hoping you can help me."
I tell her this is the second floor
the attorney is up on three.
"Charges" I feel like adding.
I've never been lucky with partners.

The Aunt's Story — a Pinewood Classic

In the words of that imperious tome,
the Berlitz Book of English by the Direct Method,
"my aunt is unmarried
and spends most of her time travelling."
The Indirect Method puts it
more tactfully, but the fact remains that my aunt,
for all her wealth, is a pitiable nomad
with no-one for company but her own sad reflection
in the polished silver of the Grand Hotel in Samarkand.
I hope that the man who jilted her
has lost his heart to a gold-digging slattern
and spends most of his time travelling
the length and breadth of his formerly safe Constituency
with the shout of "cuckold" ringing in his ears.

My aunt busies herself as a freelance journalist,
well ahead of her time, under the nom de plume
of George Peregrine. When kidnapped by bandits
in the Hindu Kush, she bears her trials
with a steely equanimity. One night by the campfire,
she gives a stirring recitation of "Dover Beach"
which leaves her captors deeply thoughtful.
When she starts to teach touch-typing
to one of her female jailers, it seems clear
that it is time for her to go. The two
racing camels and the crate of Lee-Enfields
are seen as a bargain. An unsuitable
love-affair in Smyrna, undertaken by way
of celebration, earns little attention,
but makes a deep impression on my aunt
who takes it as a vindication and an epiphany.
In the last reel, the Tory bounder
loses his nomination, offers his services

to the Liberals and is given a flea
in the ear. My aunt, primly lascivious,
is folded into the bearish arms
of the Crown Prince of Sweden.

Poirot's apprentice

A man has been gently murdered, Lady Weatherly,
a subtle but nonetheless heinous crime
and your home will have to be gently searched.
We shall treat the Sèvres collection with the greatest
respect, counting the pieces under our breath
with a minimum of handling to check the provenance.
Everyone is theoretically a suspect, even the Creator himself.
It's the police ethos, incurably sordid, but that's what we do.

You might tell your girl to set two extra places
for dinner and fetch the 1913 Chambertin from the cellar.
The Queen Charlotte Study will be quite adequate
for our Operations Room. We want to put you to
as little trouble as possible. There is no need to alter
the tenor of your lives. Mr. Catastrophe Evans,
the landscaper, can continue his visits to the
upper bedrooms to discuss his designs.
Your rows with Lord Weatherly about the inheritance
can proceed with full vigour and no fear
of interruption. We may need to speak to you
again for a routine caution. "Je regrette le dérangement"
as my colleague would say. Good man, Poirot.
Ask your daughter could I have a word? A bientôt.

While they run the titles

Ignacio Gomez brushes his sealskin hair
before taking to the night and the street.
He is living a significant moment
that waits to be taken up in the teeth
of a headline and shaken. Officer
Flaherty cleans his gun with his tongue
then puts it away. He was only fooling.
May Feinstein, younger than she looks in the novel,
wriggles into the crime-scene dress
her father warned her against. A dog
of melting-pot inheritance cocks its leg
at a hydrant then stares up its leash
at a genderless hand that means
business, wrenching the animal back
to its exercise. Was that an unusual
ring on his/her finger, something
we need to keep our eye on for later?
If we're not distracted by the soundtrack,
meanstreet percussion: sewer-grates,
blundstone boots and dustbin lids.
This might be the time to leave,
before it develops into something less
than we start to imagine, before the lips
move and we're led by the crimping nose
up the path of an overripe garden.

Comic Strip

Bazza McKenzie, innocent abroad,
dim and foul-mouthed as a drunken starlet,
drops naff mauvais mots for bed and board
(he hopes) topped up with claret and harlot
and charms South African ladies with scarlet
lips and histories in the pubs of Earls Court
with quips like: "Peace and Sports, not War and Rorts!"

a Communist slogan he saw on a sign
at the Gabba during the Springbok circus,
and "you and me? Like Elsa and the lion"
"like a sleeping sentry and a platoon of Gurkhas"
she mutters as Bazza exits to a murk as
foul and smoggy as his mates said it was
and chunders festoons like the blizzard of Oz.

Bazza looks like a bloke I went to school with
and saw sometimes in the mirror over the basin
scowling like someone you wouldn't want to fool with,
a tough full-forward called Craig or Jason
who finished the post-match booze-up with his face in
the toilet-bowl, a bloke who found women a puzzle
and belonged outdoors with a lead and a muzzle.

And look at me now, duchessed and poncey,
trying to versify in Royal Rhyme
with stanzas trippingly light and bouncy
(well, tripping over their feet). Since Chaucer's time,
this measure is seldom used for the sublime.
I could do a parody: "The Chaplain of Pentridge Gaol"
or one with possibilities: "Keith Miller's Tale".

Seeking a Sponsor

I'm an older emerging poet, like Dracula
rising from the crypt for the clock-on whistle
at five minutes to midnight, to draft a vernacular
jingle or a loosely metrified epistle
addressed to persons unknown or merely notional
on the theme and variations of the family curse,
three parts confessional and one part devotional.
I need a patron like a foundling needs a wet-nurse.

Every poet needs to find his own invoice
and pay up promptly. Your firm could meet my costs
out of petty cash. For you, it's a win-win choice:
goodwill from the Arts Community and a tax loss.
Your name and logo could sing in the hearts of my friends.
Just give me the means to dignify my ends.

We appreciate your call

a hundred and ten percent. Calls may be
monitored for quality and customer control.
Press the appropriate digit for a counsellor
fluent in one of the following dialects:
cyberbabble, victimese, solipso-exemptional,
psychopatois, derridaconian, sitcomic,
rapatonal, puffpastiche and pedanto-forensic.
Our standby music is put together
from the best of the Christmas compilation CDs
issued on a separate disc and available
at all our outlets. If you suffer from cognitive
impairment and have forgotten the reason
for your call, press hash for a service
consultant who will assist you to purchase
one of our products. Make a sandwich and a cup
of coffee, tape the phone to your ear and have
a nice day. We will be with you momentarily.

we are not alone

I type "Roswell" into the Google window
and am led by zig-zag paths to a sobering story:
Doctor Sam Fell of Broken Springs, Idaho,
after reading a letter from his wife's attorney,
did what a man has to do. He threw his pit-bull
in the back of the pick-up, loaded up Big Macs,
french fries, a crate of Schlitz, a full
palette of Tammy Wynette albums,
drove out into the plains and parked in a lay-by
under a bilious moon. Before you could say: "Stand
By Your Man" he was hooped by a ring of lights
like a Honolulu welcome. The dials on the dash panel
went ape and the whole kit and caboodle
was sucked up like fluff into a Hoover.

Sam woke in a cage of force-fields
with laser-swords probing and belabouring
every inch of his body. Twisted beings
with melting faces spoke in strange cadences,
gabbing like divorce-lawyers or East Coast pundits.
He blacked out finally, sinking into the crushed sleep
of the suddenly abducted. When he came to in the drunk-
tank of a Boise facility, he couldn't stop screaming.
Coming out of sedation, he muttered to the nurse:
"They don't need to sleep. They hover there waiting
till they feel the vibrations from one of us hurting.
And you're one of their agents. You've got the shape."

The Village of the Third Age

The fitness programme is a self-actualising paradigm
that steels the mind and goes to the heart of the matter
run by a breveted instructrix in a claret and lime
body-stocking who admits to eighty but is in fact
seventy-five and doesn't look a day over fifty.
She has survived two ex-husbands and they her
but it was a close-run thing. We start with air-lifting,
spiriting away a potentially threatening atmosphere
with languid Tai Chi movements then segue to karate,
and smash imaginary Ikea furniture to splinters.
To avoid the heat of the day, we set the alarm
for five-thirty in Summer, seven in Winter.

For the softcore self-indulgent, we have passive aerobics,
tantric shopping to ease you gently out of your savings,
an introduction to the Internet for the cyberphobic
and a lecture series on the history of crazy-paving.
Naturism is practised on non-visiting days
in the Northern barbecue-nook but there's no obligation.
The intention is merely to make a humble statement:
equal before God and Man, whatever our station.
On Sunday, the Reverend preaches in glossolalia
and we all join hands and sing: "God Bless Australia".

Rooster to Feather-Duster

The senator leads with his chin, knows no other way.
But calling the UN chief a pawn of Osama...
He got out the wrong side of the bed that day.

And his pledge of loyalty to keep the journos at bay
before there was even a hint of a back-room drama...
The senator leads with his chin, knows no other way.

And appointing a loan-shark's mistress as his new PA...
the mysterious bank-draft from Grand Bahama...
He got in bed with the wrong side that day.

He admits that a cross-bench source is in his pay.
"So what? Their secret plan will hurt the farmer!"
The senator leads with his chin, knows no other way.

Then photographed in erotic disarray
with an acrobat on a trip to Okinawa...
the senator leads with his chin, knows no other way.
He got out the side of the wrong bed that day.

Cupid O

The name "Cupid O" was on everyone's lips,
turning them to bows and cellos and bee-stung
plosions of bliss. Cupid O, whatever it was,
was coming with an unstoppable urgency
and coming soon, so the sky-writers said
and the subliminal spam-dunks that kissed
the screen for a split second, the song lyrics
of alternative bands, bloggers and twitterers
and sifters of urban myth, anywhere
outside the loop of the orthodox.

Was it a film, a video-game, a love-philtre,
a new-generation gizmo to be inserted into
that puzzling orifice in your new computer
which wasn't explained in the Manual,
the ultimate in alien devices? Rumours
spread: Cupid O was a comprehensive
dating service that could analyse millions of sites
and provide an unerring match-up in seconds;
that the source was the Russian Mafia,
launching an unending stream of Eastern
European prostitutes on world markets;
that it was a cybernetic Trojan Horse, infiltrating
a dozen glittering viruses to cripple
the Internet, in the interests, variously,
of Al Qaeda, the Chinese and following
the logic of such things, the Cubans.

No previously listed company stepped up
to claim the name. In the hiatus, a dozen
bogus companies were launched offshore
in the cubicles of drowsy Post Offices,
each sporting a name that nodded

in the given direction: "Eros X",
"ID COUP", "Bows and Arrows"
and all were over-subscribed within days
in the absence of any prospectus.

What was being sold was the absence itself,
a phantom pain from an amputated limb,
finessed away in your sleep by unseen
hands, an advance copy of an addiction
rushed off the press while the drug
was still being tested. Cupid O
could be weighed in grammes or tonnes,
valued in easy terms, in bullion or
immortal souls. In essence, it was
an essence, born from its naming,
a baboon-dance of acoustics.

The truth emerged – or did it? – that Cupid O
was a male fragrance produced in their existing
laboratory by an outlaw motorcycle gang
from the poultry-farming fringes of Sydney,
partly financed by a syndicate of Swedish
crime-writers. At worst, it was a sweetening
of grubby money or a clumsy side-stepping
of tax authorities. No hardened conspiracist
was going to be fobbed off by that. The tide
of investment surged back and forth
like a year's-end cycle pumped by a swollen moon.

A product in material form is an anti-climax,
something of another age that we have long outgrown,
too easily had and not worth waiting for.

Patriarch

The old trainer has won with lengths to spare
the Cup, the premiership and the breeder's bonus:
bred the horse, bred the mare,
bred most of the owners
and the jockey too. Gave the girl her chance
and stuffed the handicappers.
With the three-kilo claim, led them a merry dance
in the last 200, went like the clappers.

He would like to thank nobody
in particular. Maybe the missus
for minding her own business and perhaps God
for making him hard but never vicious.
He is one of a kind in a small universe.
He'll write his own elegy. He'd like to drive the hearse.

A Fable

In the later refinements of the purge
every shape and faction of neutrality
is swept away. The apathetic
are made to care, the blind given eyes
to weep with, the lame fresh legs to make
a dash for the border. The old nobility
feign madness more plausibly than most.
Ministers outdo each other in zealotry
so they won't be gaps in next year's photograph.
Office-holders of the Writers' Collective
search for le mot juste to clinch their confessions.
Revisionist historians, of their own accord,
don peasant dress to hoe the campus lawns.
Functionaries passed over for promotion
hide their children in cellars or advise their wives
to sue for divorce for their own protection.
For those hitched to a falling star, suicide
is the last word in preventive medicine.

It is six months before the absence
of the reclusive President is noticed.
He has fled with his mistress, his dwarf/confidant
and the last pickings from the Treasury
to a fortified sanatorium high above
the fetid reach of extradition.
But the eyes of his every image
still follow you around the room,
a triumph of Peoples' Portraiture.

Surrounding states that might have been tempted
to fatten themselves on their sick neighbour
keep their distance as from a site of contagion.
With no common foe to concentrate their minds

the tide of denunciation ebbs slowly.
The survivors, all with blood on their hands,
drag themselves inch by inch into a zone
of quiet contemplation. In a land stripped
of innocence, truth and reconciliation
seem like a misalliance. After a year,
a whisper finds its way through a pair of lips:
"Let this be a lesson to us all."
Under the old prescription, he who dares
to speak first must dare to lead. But another
whisper opens out into the first dissenting
voice since the time of a million flowers,
too long ago to remember:
"Let's make an end to lessons. We need
a generation of slow and steady growth,
a time of forgetting and being forgotten."

H.H. deals with the media

"I'm a guy who loves women. I'm a romantic."
—Hugh Hefner on the occasion of his eighty-third birthday.
"The word 'romantic' has come to mean so many things that, by itself, it
means nothing at all."
—A.O. Lovejoy (sic)

You want me to expand on that? Well, I might
surprise you. I'm not just a pretty face.
I know my "isms" and not only the monosyllabic
one on the tip of your tongue, young man!
OK. I'm not a neo-platonist or a late
pre-Raphaelite. Byron has some appeal,
I admit, but my own monomania
is a little sunnier. Keats makes me think
of pale loitering in an age before sunlamps.
A springtime ramble in the manner
of Wordsworth would play merry hell
with my allergies. I'll content myself
with the image of Joylene from September
1967, admiring the floral prints in a
draper's window, a child of nature
teetering on the brink of fashion.

 Professor Lovejoy concluded after 20,000 words
that Romanticism is best defined by what it isn't:
Realism. The kitchen-sink. Skin blemishes.
Body-hair. Childbirth. An operation
to remove the prostate. The grim reaper.
I refer you all to my editorial from the Seventies:
"Playboy and the New Humanism". Do we still
export bibles to the Third World? We know what
they'd prefer. Even in Kandahar. Especially in Kandahar.
I'll finish with a line from Keats to save

you hours of web surfing for a cute tag-line:
"And what is Love? It is a doll dressed up"
or not as the case may be. That's a wrap.

Anchor of Current Affairs

She's an ear for heights and an eye for sore sights
a shoulder to sling a designer bag on
a head for figures and a bum for tights
and lashes like a trannie with drag on.

Her make-up trailer has a make-up trailer
her PA a PA and her nanny a nanny,
she calls the Defence Chief "hello sailor"
and the PM "my sweet little manny".

"If she's a journalist, I'm a tart!"
says the boss of the rival channel.
She isn't. He is. And he gave her her start
hosting his Good Morning panel.

Death by Wikipedia

Caesar had three regular doubles, each
as perfect a likeness as any to be found
on a fresh-minted coin from the Treasury,
down to the finest detail of gout or calvity,
plus a dozen part-timers for distance shots:
tribunalia, podia, high altars et cetera.

The regulars, known simply as Primus,
Secundus and Tertius, by order of recruitment,
had a list of specific duties:
Primus was a food-taster and qualified toxicologist.
Secundus had to sleep with Calpurnia, a short
straw he never stopped whining about
but the lady herself, though not above
suspecting something, made no complaint.
Tertius had to share the Dictator's own bed,
a narcissistic fantasy Caesar had always coveted.

It was, in fact, Secundus who went
to the Senate on that fateful Ides of March.
"Don't go", said Calpurnia, "whoever you are.
Your aura looks a bit unsure of itself."
But he went of course and it ended badly.

So what of Caesar himself? A populist historian
claims that the Dictator, long secretly addicted
to Oriental mysticism, made good his escape
in the company of Tertius and sought the good life
far to the East of the Roman dominion, learning
the hundred steps to selfless oblivion. The course
of the Roman world to the sorry outcome of Actium
was a simple case of mistaken identity.

Facebook

Your deck of cards has an extra suit called "friends",
in the language of the software but not your own.

They are named but mostly unmet, some inexistent
as likely as not, lacking dimension and history

and also that unedited quality
of contact on the wing and a tactility

that might be unsafe. "Would you like to be my friend?"
is an invitation you haven't heard in years

from a plaintive newcomer in nursery-school
or a man in a park ventriloquising a puppy.

Your on-screen suitors talk with a clipped inelegance
and like to watch: fictions meshing and unravelling,

the dynamism of the sensual world contained
in a mouse-scuttle. They are an Otherworld

that can be leached out of this one
like dead constituents rising to vote again.

The Stand-Up Psychiatrist

Did you hear about
the discombobulated hobgoblin
the baby elf centre
the gnome away from Nome
the pygmy who felt belittled
the ten-inch pianist?
Do you sometimes think
that people are looking d

                    o

                 w

              n

              t

                 h

                    e

                    i

                       r

                       n

                       o

                    s

                    e

                 s

                          at you ?
What do you find on a three-foot couch?
My patients. I'm a shrink. That's what I do.
I'm just making small talk here
to put you at your ease
and your p's and q's
your dotted t's and your crossed i's:
an alphabet soup just like
your Mama used to make.
Look at this watch and take deep breaths.
It's a Rolex, top of the range.
How can I afford this? You'll find out

at the end of the month. But I'm
not one of those sloths that
doodle on a pad and say nothing.
I'm proactive, an active pro.
Such a look on your face!
"Bloody hell! I thought I had a problem!"
You've taken the first step. Lighten
up and stay there. See you
next Thursday, the matinee session.

Only Money

Money is no longer an object
that jinks and rustles in the hand
in geometrical shapes that ape

the closed circuits of lust.
It used to be scarred by teeth
and petty sabotage, to smell

of leather and thieves' fingers
till it learned to swim
in widening circles of abstraction

and cycle over electronic highways.
It needs to be roughed up and
scuffed again, its bar-codes

broken and tossed, its metal strips
twisted in parrot-beaks, re-tooled
into whip-tips and tongue-ties,

tongs and ferryman's fares
so the poor would know it again
for the bad penny it always was,

brass from muck and muck from brass,
plain as a brown paper-bag
plain as a death-rattle.

tactile

snicking the ends off snow-peas with a fingernail
cuticles slipping over polished frogskin

wedging the haft of a knife in the heel of your hand
as you worry the flange off a butter-pumpkin

chopping onions in a fizz and drip of hand-eye
coordination   the cool handshake of a pork-fillet

on its final journey   the papery shiver of garlic-skin
the stubble-kiss of a choko fresh from the vine

the bite of splinters from a broom-handle
as you bash the smoke-alarm till it shuts up

the mudpie-ooze of potato-cake mixture between
your thumbs   the sticky redolence smearing the plastic

as you pick up the throbbing phone   the insinuating
caress of a velvety voice from a distant call-centre

spreading the silken cloth of a once-in-a-lifetime
opportunity   to blister the air with curses

your fingers whispering through your wife's hair
learning the shape of her skull

and the dark geography of the hemisphere
that holds the secret of balancing

a dozen tasks in the course of a morning
with a funambulist's sang-froid and poise.

Crossing

Six cyclists wait at a level-crossing,
three couples or something more random,
leaning into definition or from it.
This is a cinematic moment, asking
for a full treatment, a story to embed
itself in, or one of those shy epiphanies
needing a grand event to snap-freeze
it into poignancy. Your mind plays
with a hint of a sound-track, a faint beat
of helicopter-blades building to a hot breath
of threat or the distant but pervasive
roaring of cyclone or tsunami.

In the trick of a light-shift, the cycles
melt into horses, the riders sprout cabbage-tree
hats, their fingers fuse into gun-barrels
and the saddle-bags bulge with bibles.
You are sweating through an old and alien
skin, watching a catastrophe cantering
cheerfully up to greet you. This is what
idle moments are for, to ramble through narratives
or have them ramble through us: lyrical,
careless, innocent of any notion of pity.

Colonist

Mutton-chop whiskers around a Beef Wellington face.
He keeps a log of sins like a breviary
recited daily as a hedge against forgetting
or a ring of siege-works around an act of Grace:

flayed hides of hominoids and strange mammals
killed and embarked for scientific purposes,
towns named after mistranslated curses
involving female relatives, fleas and camels.

Yes, that was in another country and besides...
the language and all those who knew
the codes and roots from which it grew,
have fed on their own livers, sickened and died.

A culture has an insensate life of its own.
Watch it squirming on slides under a microscope.
It needs the gaze of the lettered interloper
to be catalogued among the named and known.

It wasn't meant as a pillage of souls
but a requisition and a reassignment,
a realignment of the heart's priorities
to carve Your Name on tombs and begging-bowls.

Spider Solitaire

is played with four full suits of Spades
Death's army-camp with palissades
of raven-beaks and black mambas
for tired saints and desperate gamblers
        that's Spider Solitaire

in nursing-homes the game that's played
in lieu of prayer or mess-parade
when life has lost all sap and timbre
and lights are always stuck on amber
        that's Spider Solitaire

when memories dissolve and fade
and minds are lost or just mislaid
whose is the face gone tense and sombre?
there's just one round left in the chamber
one final bend and uphill grade
        that's Spider Solitaire

Ivan

A Russian woodsman had most of his face
scooped away like porridge from a bowl
by a big brown bear. He was lucky enough, or not,
to survive as an object of pity and horror to all
but a few cosmetic surgeons who saw him
as a challenge and a ticket to fame.
They had to start from scratch and bite
that gave them a blank canvas to work on,
space for a masterpiece made of struts
and impasto, a face that no genetic
lottery could ever throw up, the face
of a matinee idol or a mask of gravitas,
paterfamilias of his people, the full
incarnation of the Slavonic Soul.

The Socialist Realists among the surgeons
were ousted after a coup and the Petersburg
Spring left a new Master of the College
of a humanist persuasion. He gave the woodsman
Pushkin's eyebrows and the nose of Diaghilev.
The shattered chin was shored up into a form
worthy of bearing the beard of Tolstoy.
The original eyes, left mostly undamaged,
still held a darting, untrustful glance.
He persuaded the subject to wear corrective
lenses and train his gaze to a steady
but sensitive repose, like the orbs of Shostakovitch.

Ivan's role as the new Homo Post-Sovieticus
was a poor fit. He spurned the offers of every
political party with a deep-rooted peasant
suspicion and refused to tour North America
with the surgeon, approving only a brief

documentary film. Determined to face his demons,
he joined a circus as an animal-wrangler
and bear-whisperer, moving the brutes to tears
with the full weight of his forgiveness.
His only trip outside of Mother Russia
was a visit to Poland to meet the family
of a comely illusionist from Cracow,
a colleague and friend and perhaps a little more.

This unfamiliar brush with tenderness
and the monumental quality of his face
filled Ivan with a need to mould his life
into something it had never been.
He learned to read more fluently,
to play the balalaika. He replaced
the rotting timbers of the village school
at his own expense and gave comfort and alms
to the poor, the sick and downtrodden.

But when a Patriarch proposed his village
as a site of pilgrimage, Ivan felt
the various elements of his sculpted lineage
ripple and twist into the birthing
of a new National Wisdom. All he allowed
was the inclusion of his name in a modest
Litany that would give no offence and be read
only once a year, on his mother's birthday.

Blue

You stare into a sky of an ever-reaching blue
deep as your prior notion about it, furred sepia
round the edges from traces of fires or the slow creep
of macular degeneration. The affective shading
is for each his own business, colour of Summers past
when time slowed to a hackney canter or a Provencal
ramble through heathland of mimosa and lavender.
This is the blue you set off into on the upswing
of your life, with no sense of destination or gravity,
the blue whose immensity shrinks your every mistake,
sets no limit to your travels or callow meditations:
on the need to unlearn to believe your eyes, the need
for time to sway to the rhythm of the senses, on the nature
of blue, on the nature of nature, on the blue of blue.

The Last Hour

No time to walk the rainforest if it were there.
And outside isn't the best place to be.
Waste no time on regrets, apologies
or last messages. Make a simple checklist,
the senses, say, and be loosely methodical.

For the eyes, scenes from a film that can express
an essence in ten minutes, something painterly,
where the mind of the artificer reminds you
constantly of its presence; to the spiritual,
something like the real world.

For the ears, four minutes of the Ravel
string quartet, then two minutes
of silence for remembered birdsong.

For the nose, truffle-oil, sandalwood,
a smoke-damaged Gallimard edition
of "A la Recherche du Temps Perdu".

A simple meal of grilled trumpeter
with lemon and garlic butter,
something green – an artichoke heart?
a dessert of a single strawberry
and the 2003 Riesling from Freycinet.

On tactility, I suggest nothing but a smile.
I am of that generation that draws the curtains.
And you, my love, are synaesthesia in motion
and in repose. Sans toi, sans quoi que ce soit.

No time for reading, but perhaps a simple precis
of everything. We will think of three unanswerable
questions, ask them and wait quietly for as long as it takes.

on empty

On a hot day the North-West Plain is so flat it isn't.
The horizon curves and stirs like a wisp of moustache.
Animals burrow that aren't meant to burrow.
Prey walk past their predators under a white flag.
The eyes of roadkill are left to boil in their sockets.
The can of beer is dry when you open it.
A cigarette is rolling another swagman.
The motor smokes nervously before you start it.
The mobile phone sweats, whimpers and croaks.
The devil is on holiday in Tasmania.
The paddock on the left is Texas.
The seat of government is the only tree.
We'll take a rest-stop at the next mirage.
Is it far? It has been. Are we there yet? No.

From *Duck Soup & Swansongs*
(Ginninderra Press 2018)

Individual Agreement

Sir, about the clause in my contract
that says I will need to have a limb amputated
to enhance my visual and affective impact
for the street-corner phone-plan sales team:
I have a question.
Do I get severance pay?

A Catholic Boyhood (condensed)

So you think you've lost your Faith...
Did it have your name on it?

How many times, son, how many times?
You boastful little sod!

Nominy Dominy Hominy Deuteronomy
Give up self-abuse and astronomy.

Ten Hail Marys round the oval.

Australian Poetry 1850-1945

When gullies were dales and creeks were brooks
there were four-figure sales for poetry books.
When the woods went bush with the swags and blackfellas
the poetry push became best-sellers
till the time was ripe for the clever blokes
and the only rich tripe was a five-star hoax.
Then depression and war seemed permanent fixtures
and most of the punters had gone to the pictures.

Set 'em up Joe

It's a bar like any other in downtown Storyville.
The animals talk and the men have speech impediments

or bad accents, like the Englishman, Irishman and Scot
or the rabbi, the priest and the mufti who drink together

when they're not walking three abreast down an unnamed street
behind three golfers who are always par for the course.

"Doctor, doctor, I think it's some sort of seizure!"
"Computer, books and papers? It's the Fraud Squad."

"Make mine a double entendre" says the chantoozie.
"The Senator will have the usual" says the floozie.

Captain's Pick Haiku

the worst cabinet
since Doctor Caligari
great team be buggered

Another Day at the Office

He winds up like a pitcher on the mound
then signs a voluminous piece of paper

as if the training-wheels are still attached
to his arm   inspects the Praetorian Guard,

weeds out one whose eyebrows dance
another who looks dangerously proactive

time for a couple of executive tweets
from the lounge at the airfield   then off

to a golf course in the Emirates
with the world's largest bunker

where his own name shimmers in
mega-lights that can be seen from Space.

He needs to be seen to be being something.

Seven Channels

In the credits of a crime thriller
set in the swamps of Louisiana:
"bait-buckets by Leon de Ponce
Sporting Hire of Lafayette"

Fashions-in-the-Field at the Spring Carnival:
a hat like an avian pile-up in a wind-tunnel.
A colourful Racing Identity tells his partner's cleavage
the joke about the blind steeplechaser.

At the Eurovision Song Contest
the drummer in the Taras Bulba outfit
is a tap or two behind the beat
as if the others started without him.

The celebrity chef dips a manicured finger
into the crème brûlée then licks it.
She's never seen an apron outside of a threesome
with her New York agent and the French maid.

An author shows off his new dental implants
to the Book Club and explains himself:
"There's no bibliography. This is a self-help book.
I knew it all because the voices told me."

A super-mum on the Board of Chase Manhattan
has a twin-berth jogging-pram with five-speed gears
and a Monza racing-stripe. She tells her nanny she
should do something with her hair. You can have it all.

In the last reel of a heist-caper movie
A brace of body-doubles sort each other out
on a loot-strewn bed in a collage of oiled limbs.
The room has windows that look out on to the unattainable.

You liked it when they showed the mother kangaroo
putting the joey to bed, then the test pattern.
It was out of your hands somehow. Now the screen
just goes black at a touch. A quiet flatlining.

The Quick Brown Fox

"The quick brown fox jumps over the lazy dog"
is a found poem of sorts in a lyric metre
fit for a Tyrolean walking-song and, of course,
an efficient pangram with few repetitions
and no strain on the syntax. It is also
a popular success without peer, better known
than any line of Yeats, Auden or even the Bard.
As a child, I traced it on a slate till my fingers stiffened
and it filled the nightmares of millions of blindfolded typists.

Like many another masterpiece, it was penned by A. Nonymous
or U.N. Certain, though many names have been whispered,
from Albert the Prince Consort to Ho Chi Minh.
More likely, it was some brisk entrepreneur
of the pre-post-industrial Age, like a Pitman
of shorthand fame or one of his clerks
in a false collar and an eyeshade
or perhaps there is truth in the Stalinist claim
that a Cyrillic version evolved from the struggles
of the Dactylographic Collective of downtown Tblisi.

We are learning again to shrink from Romantic excess
and see the poetic "I" as a pre-Raphaelite self-pleasurer
or, at very least, a florid North American in a bow tie.
So let us pause to honour the authors
of "the quick brown fox" et cetera.
Lucky it wasn't mauled by some brutalist editor
who liked to strip out articles and adjectives
till it all sounded like the name of a Navajo chief.

Balloons

The Montgolfier brothers made their first serious essay
with a billowing globe of specialty paper and taffeta
that bore in a basket their first nervous passengers:

a sheep called Climb-To-The-Sky, a duck and a rooster
but although the globe with its buttoned-up panels
burst on impact like a libertine's pantalon,

the creatures emerged intact and were granted,
no doubt, a ticket-of-leave from the abattoir,
perhaps a royal pension. The balloons were designed

partly with a mind to overfly fortresses
and empty on the foreign jackals below
what nuisances the cash-strapped nation could afford:

baskets of oath-affirming arms, talking heads,
crushing didactic tableaux and sharpened clausulae
which might unman them and force a surrender

but worked better, in the end, against each other,
death by rhetoric and gesture, a grand guignol
theatricality with an iron-filing stench of blood

till the balloons came into their own as a
narrative device for reactionary novelists
who filled the baskets with stiff-lipped Pimpernels

powdered wigs and tear-stained décolletages
soaring to safety over the cliffs of Dover.
History as bunk, History as hissy fits in the wings

of the Comédie and the ranks of the gutter Press,

History as the slap and chop in the waves of
happenstance, History as a highway with slow lanes,

passing lanes, roadblocks, bottlenecks and steaming
heaps of roadkill and with luck, surveillance from the sky
and a flyover corridor for endangered species.

Anargasm

A poem that rides on its own melting
in slipstream mode to a wet nothing

is entropism, the long downtime at a
tight impasse, an indolent motor we

don't prime-heat. A soon-wilting stem
wants re-setting. The lampoon idiom

wanes on a tone-timer stoplight, dim-
lit grid, phoneme waste-station M on

the planet Moi, emitting no words as
a poem that rides on its own melting.

Note: Each line of the poem is an anagram of the first line.

Report from the circuit judge

of the Mountain View Rhododendron and Arts Festival
Poetry Competition:

A bewildering mixture of subjects and styles
much harder to judge than the sheep-dog trials.
"When he picked that one, he must have been pissed!"
you'll say, I suppose, but here's the short-list:

a mother coping with hyperactive three-year-old quintuplets;
a recipe for gluten-free muffins in rhyming couplets;
a plea for Middle Eastern fences to be mended;
a dark and inscrutable sonnet – Highly Commended;
a concrete poem that made the line-count problematical;
a II O pastiche entirely in formulas mathematical;
a page of fortune-cookie philosophy like a hash-head praying
(I know who wrote that one but I'm not saying);

To compensate for the many Dear Departeds
for the lovers too bold or too faint-hearted,
there's a Baby Boom in the entries, some even in wedlock.
A society firmly rooted down to the bedrock.
So I've given First Prize to the beleaguered mother.
I'll send this off and then I might have another.

From the Gonzo Dictionary of Literary Terms

bugarstice

is the name of a verse form sung
by Dalmatian shepherds to their sheep
as an instrument of forced conversion
or to calm them during the rigours
of drenching and cleansing. It is a formal
measure characterised by the obligatory
caesura after the seventh syllable
that echoes the halt at nightfall
of combats against Turk or Bulgarian
or the exhaustion of sated troubadours
after their "doux combats" with well-muscled
milkmaids. It is not to be confused
with the "bucolic diaeresis" that resulted
from excessive consumption of fermented
sour apples, the "Barnstaple tarantella"
of the famous passage from Chaucer.

Brett and Arthur

Whiteley in the Rimbaud museum at Charleville,
naked, with a photo of the poet covering his face,
something of a larrikin touch to the homage,
good-humoured worlds away from the shit-on-God graffito
that Arthur would daub on walls around the drab town
he had to boomerang back to when he ran out of cash.

Nothing surprising at first in the lure of Rimbaud:
the flammable property of poetry, Art as an all-up bet,
ambitions beyond the station of any art or craft,
the siren-song of transgression, absinthe and hashish
as a leg-up to climb out of yourself into something
that would see the big picture, be the big picture.

In his own portrait of Rimbaud, Whiteley doesn't stray far
from the only clear photograph of the young poet
and fills most of the canvas with a rendering
of emanations from the poet's brain. Partial inventory:
rounded hillocks and boulders, a white staircase
curving and tapering back into yellow sand, in the distance,

a rearing shark with the hint of a quivering buttock,
a mouth like a hammerhead vulva and something
that looks like the island of Doctor Moreau. Brett's
copied-out passages from Rimbaud might suggest only
a cursory reading but the details of the picture
point to a strong grasp of motifs and sources.

I have seldom found the surrealist mode disturbing
where the psyche seems to reach out to the ambient world.
There is often a lush efflorescence in the works,
more fluid and dynamic than the clinging shapes,
the stalled moves and furred textures of nightmare. Here,
there's a South-Seas sunniness that undoes Arthur's ferocity.

For the better perhaps. And Whitely's other representation
of Arthur? The sculpture of two huge matches, one live, one dead?
I must have blinked and missed the flare in between. Or I needed
warmth in my life, not a conflagration. A lost weekend
in Hell was season enough and illumination best dammed
and released in a steady trickle of lucidity.

Brett asked the question about Van Gogh: "is Art worth a life?"
The answer for me is "no" if it didn't need to be. So what
do you do when you're not delirious? Arthur:
"I set myself up as an exemplary burnt-out case
 and mind a shop in a hell-hole in Africa." Brett:
"I roll down my sleeves and get on with the job."

Theatre

In Zuckmayer's "The Captain of Köpenick" an ex-general,
now Kommandant of a Prussian prison, has a company of
toothless old lags riding brooms up a ramp to re-enact
a famous cavalry charge: "Ah, my brave lads!"
drools the ancient general, "What a fine body of men!"

In a Brendan Behan play, a stage direction:
a nun in full habit shuffles on to the scene and in one
swift movement, removes the habit to reveal
a man in a shabby suit who informs the audience:
"I'm a secret policeman and I don't care who knows it!"

From Joe Orton: a young expectant mother
without benefit of wedlock, is counselled by a woman
Social Worker of sinister gentility and born-again smugness:
"Now don't get me wrong. There is no more beautiful sight
than two young married people making love."

From Howard Barker, a scene set in the vault
of the newly established Bank of England: a dissipated
Charles II, a louche mistress, a wide-boy cockney courtier
and the sudden irruption of a furious Yorkshire merchant:
"Piece of paper be buggered! I want to see my money, I want to touch
it!"

Howard Barker again. A conference in the Kremlin:
Churchill, Stalin, a nervous foul-mouthed interpreter
and a bewildered Scottish comedian. (Stalin has been
misinformed that Churchill loves Scottish comedians.)
"I can't fucking translate that! This bastard will kill us all!"

An Oz sample? Not easy. Dead-pan lines. Have to be there.
From Williamson: the middle-aged son tells his father that
he has just left his wife for his mistress. That night, the old dad
catches him in flagrante on the sofa with yet another woman,
half his age. The patriarch shakes his head: "Just not good enough, son."

Financial Adviser's Report

The Company has a web site of course.
In fact, it is a web site pure and simple
with a listing on the Bucharest Bourse
to try to put a backside on the pimple.
There's a fleet of trucks from various lines
for sundry goods to fall off the back of
and escort cuties dressed up to the nines
booking gigs from a boarding-house in Cracow.

The CEO is a paintball sniper
and MBA in powerpoint presentations,
tucking dodgers under your windscreen-wiper
and starting phone-calls with "congratulations!".
Unless your greed for profit is obsessive,
note that the risk assessment reads "aggressive".

The Defence Sums Up

He couldn't have used his car. They were fixing the steering.
The mysterious red traces turned out to be herring.
So here's a man who entertained thoughts of murder?
The complete reverse is true. Componite verba.
The prosecution case is a catalogue of failure.
The suspicious van was the 7 NEWS make-up trailer.
The Crown's star witness, the aptly-named Miss Farrago,
under pressure, shifted and rolled like an unsecured cargo.
On the night in question, an unshakable alibi:
my client met with the Prime Minister. Would he lie ?
Unexplained sightings in bizarre places, juicy snippets
of gossip ? Elementary. My client is a known triplet.
And the empty grave was disturbed from the inside out.
Would you say that constitutes reasonable doubt?

Chairborne

The Treasurer sifts and sorts
his cherry-picked data, rorts

the stats, projections and parameters,
poses at his desk for the news cameras

then does his sums, the only part of the job
he studied for: how much change from the two bob

his mum gave him to go to the corner shop,
how many years take his pension to the top

scale before he quits. Pity the rates are pegged
to those of the civil service, the dregs

left over from the binges of the other team
before they were tipped from office, who seem

to love answering questions you don't ask
and fail to understand that the real task

is selling the budget, not shaping it.
Sell punters a pup and it takes two years to wake up to it.

Comfort Stop

Friedensreich Hundertwasser
is a name that comes not trippingly
off a Maori or pakeha tongue
yet he was the pride of Kawakawa
and a Living Treasure of New Zealand,
an internationally known ecologist
and architect and above all,
in the popular mind, the Klimt of the khazi,
creator of the world's most charming
and beautiful toilet-block.

a chef d'oeuvre of Loo Art Deco,
columns and arches that marry
a Mad King Ludwig kitsch
to the frosty decadence
of Viennese orientalism,
plus a nod to the Alice in Wonderland
embrace of a crazy-paved world.
There's also a sense of the Antipodean
flair for ad hoc improvisation,
unlikely local materials that come to hand,
the co-option of workers given a chance
to exercise their crafts and tours de main.

It's a tourist hub, approached by a tiptoed
sword-dance through flailing selfie-sticks.
The trompe l'oeil windows, necessarily opaque,
are bottles in pastel shades like lime, puce
and lavender. The asymmetrical tiles evoke the slow
deliberation of the builder of a drystone wall
but the symphony of shapes and colours
has all the sophistication of a painter's practised eye
that takes the artless layman's breath away.

In the off-season, it must be a focus
for the locals, a comfort and convenience
stop for polite gossip, hard to conceive of
the other kind in such an ambience.
Imagine a Clochemerle pissoir sunny-side up:
no sinister rendez-vous, no political
cabals or vicious rumours. The spiritual
force of Hundertwasser lingers still.

Latitudes

Rimbaud in Paris, reeking
of anisette and slept-in tatters,
makes sheep's-eyes at his betters,
wolf's-eyes at his peers.

Malcolm Lowry in Mexico,
eyes like lava, nose erupting,
smells of sulphur, cactus and lemon,
a talent that feeds on its own combustion.

Faulkner, a steadier role-model,
not on the jigger-scale but socially.
He doesn't get out much, probably
can't make it to the door.

Auden in New York, a cannier
pact with the devil, carousing at night
but never on an empty stomach,
then stoked on uppers, working all day.

Such were my thoughts when in 1968
in Marseille, I was helped up off the floor
by a regal Ghanaian prostitute and told that I
was a disgrace to the English-speaking community.

Red-Eye Flight

A numbing twelve-hour flight and at the end of it
my first scheduled appointment, a funeral:
a friend from an earlier life, seen a few months ago
on a brief visit. She stayed for just a week,
long enough to make a new nest for herself
in the bric-a-brac of my habits and attachments.
There was no physical intimacy, just a quiet
stripping-back to an almost blank page
under all the smudges and erasures.
Then she flew away to die in another hemisphere.

Albertine was the French assistante of a college
in Bristol. I saw her in the down time between classes
reading a tattered paperback with rhythmic nods
of her head, like a jazz buff pecking at the offbeat.
It was a Malraux novel, a favourite of mine. I asked
what she thought of the story of the tram conductor,
who cares nothing for politics, taken for a combatant
by the Falangists because of the strap-mark on his shirt.
As he faces the firing-squad, he makes a fist and shouts:
"Venceremos!" Was this a lesson in how to die or how
to live or just an arm of honour for the apostles of death?

I remember us drifting arm-in-arm from a party,
discussing the rift between Sartre and Merleau-Ponty.
We took our foreplay seriously in those days.
At year's-end, Albertine was off to Algeria
to join her father, a medical coopérant with a
UN team. As the time grew closer we began
to bicker like children past their bedtime.
My last words to her were the tired formula:
"Soigne-toi". Look after yourself. There was

a brittleness about her at the time and where
she was going wasn't the safest place in the world.

No contact for thirty years except by mail. I try
to imagine a different trajectory for my life
that I seem to have watched glide past like a
passenger in a train with his back to the engine.
A ten-year relationship that stuttered to a stop
for which I was found guilty in my emotional
absentia. Some weekend excursions to bohemia.
A few hare-brained adventures that cost me
less than I deserved. Albertine once did a burlesque
reading of my palm. Her verdict: "a wistful
viciousness that will never amount to much."

The in-flight movie is a slow comedy
with space to doze between the semaphoring of a joke
and its forced landing. Even the shallowest dream
can stop bad faith in its tracks: I seem to see
the celebrity faces from the picture clues
of the Giant Crossword turn into figures from a
book on marine biology: sea urchins, stingers,
Medusae. And among them the face of Albertine
fresh from the shower, her hair in wet strings,
her eyes enormous, searching me out.
Was her absence always to be the last word?

In the next fitful sleep, my unconscious has rushed
ahead to beat me to the funeral. We hear the eulogy
rolled out: a life of scholarship and public service.
I meet Albertine's daughter and a grand-daughter
aged ten. The dark eyes and metaphysical emphasis
of her grandmother. She asks me: "Who are you?"

From the Gonzo Film Archive

U.S. Military Intelligence in full evolution
from exploding cigars and toxic wetsuits
designed for Fidel to staring at goats

disarmingly till their horns drop off
or wrapping themselves in a full-body bubble
of invisibility by flexing the toned muscles

of the psyche, the way a three-year-old plays
hide-and-seek by standing in the middle
of a paddock with his eyes shut (hiding)

or open instead of counting to fifty (seeking).
The liaison officer from Noosa suggests that
none of this would work on brush turkeys

who just keep coming down the aisle of
the supermarket making for the popcorn.
There are background flashes of J. Edgar Hoover

in a tutu, Patton in his invisible bubble of
competence, Colin Powell covering his eyes
so George W. won't find him and ask him

to please explain. From slapstick to Zen and back
in a pulsating diorama. I feel like a fly on the wall,
the prototype with the tiny camera, shooting sparks.

A walk through of Anish Kapoor

(Museum of Contemporary Art: Sydney 2013)

As I pace past the stainless-steel surfaces
of the "S Curve", my two hydrocephalic heads
melt and merge into each other, then lose themselves
in my spreading shoulders. I start to burrow
into familiar phrases: "I felt the ground shift
under my feet" "this is how it looks from where I stand"
and think how easily the world slips its libretto,
is knocked sideways by illness or trickery with optics.
I search for words to frame the philosophical
question the brochure invites me to ask: how the self
can curdle, separate or drain away into
the gaze of others, how its singularity
can be taken for granted by no-one else
who doesn't have a privileged sense of its history.

At "My Red Homeland" I see tons of wax
the colour of clotting blood, worried at clock-speed
by a motorised half-caliper, tipped with a steel
cube the size of a small container on a ship's deck.
I have a stomach that thinks like a stomach, easily
unsettled by a crushing weight of stimulus.
The robotic march of metal through soft matter
evokes the slow-motion, stylised violence
of films that ask me to reach back through artifice
and distancing to the roots of empathy, a swift sense
of being gutted by proxy. I try to guess how many
truckloads of visual metaphor it took to make this,
then baulk at shaping a philosophical question
too easy to pose and too hard to answer.
I look again at the circular creep of metal,
plough or military tank, through red earth ready

for seeding or the mud of battlefields, layers
of graveyards and vanished cities, a soil fertilised
by the dissolution of forgotten lives. I am now
in the actuarial zone where life starts to shrink
into the boutique theatre of kin and friends
where you chase memories uphill to a tipping-point
of breathlessness before they start to chase you
with minds of their own. Your navel-contemplation
is a way of logging in to the wheel of existence
where off-cuts of information peel away like
the flecks and ribbons of red clay. It's all about
the journey, getting to nowhere elegantly, naked.

Horn

I look at Bernie McGann's saxophone
left on the stand in the break between sets
inert and unresolved like a question-mark
uncoupled from a very important question
and tumbled on its back   all bumps and
corrugations like its owner's face and the same
ginger-snap colour with the sheen rubbed off
the bell gaping like a death-mask   the greenish
tinge of a long wasting disease stealing
over its lips   waiting   like an old dog tied up
outside a pub for its master to shuffle out
and take it for a final lollop in the park
put it through its larrikin paces and old tricks.

Branford Marsalis: Concert in New Orleans

The notes hit the receptors and spread
sweet confusion, a multi-media event
beneath the grizzled canopy of my skull,
scum on a bayou surface and bubbles under,
fried catfish and tabasco freeing their scents
to frisk in the glades and thickets of my head.
Frets and stops and keys dance rainbows
that tell no stories beyond the chassé
of their own elegant acrobatics,
like the sift and winkle-pick of mathematics,
pure and sufficient only unto the day.
At the end of the set, applause like hailstones.

Jazz music recollected in tranquility
is a contradiction or two in terms
or a hoop-snake that swallows itself whole,
from wheel to microdot as it stops rolling.

Dream Homes

In my dreams I have often tapped into
the false memory of homes where I have never lived,
slapped together from a kit of architectural
and narrative clichés: a harbourside flatette
with no definable features but outside stairs
and a dresser filled with unsecured secrets;
a spacious open-plan apartment with an
indoor garden tended by unseen hands;
a two-storey terrace with upstairs rooms
which were never used, all lounges and libraries
with not a bedroom in sight. And none
of these homes was a primary residence,
all bolt-holes to escape to, safe houses
to hide the residue of unnamed crimes,
places to bring an unsuitable lover to
or work on the draft of an explosive memoir.

A diet of crime and espionage fiction might
explain the building blocks but not the impulse.
An analyst might look for an unhappy child
with a self that fitted badly which he needed
a weekend retreat away from. The social realist
might posit something sterner and more mundane:
a North Shore Sydney boy obsessed with
real estate options. Who would have thought?

Perhaps it's just a random playing-out of our
common condition: homo somnifaciens
who needs doors opening on to other lives
and possibilities or a transfer station for psychic
waste and old embarrassments. Dream homes
might be a free translation of the well-known
dream of flying, clear of that other dream

of a long corridor that debouches into another day
or not, like a bird dreaming of not flying.

Guard Duty

This side of my eyelids is a dark that lacks
density, matt patches of light tempering
the spread of shadow, wrinkles of glass-shatter

frozen just short of a drop, a millimetre
of airy perspective with a hint of
comic-book stars that follow a knock-out punch

or the thirty-six candles of the French
translation from the graphic, a black and white
negative of the New Year pyrotechnics,

son et lumière, fridge-hum and a faint spill
of streetlight. Bonne Année indeed, bonnier
than the last one or the one before, if I lived

my life backwards or were legally blind
to all the evidence. I wait for sleep to shut
the world off like a falconer's hood.

The composer turns to the camera

windows of a soul well-schooled
in nuance and discrimination.
He wears the cravat, vest
and sharkfin lapels of his age
and class. The white beard,
combed and fluffed, half-hides
lips that promise to gather
into a faint moue of diffidence
in the face of this clapping
contraption and its hooded keeper.
"They think" he thinks, "to capture
an Age on the wing, like netting
a butterfly. But I know better.
'exegi monumentum perennius aere'
A man who knew about brass
and wood-winds and the strings
of Orpheus, music to buzz
in the ears of a thousand
generations. Voilà."
Done. A minor inconvenience
quickly forgotten.

His music more slowly forgotten
but fading, the name already
with the whiff of a footnote about it.
He is teetering, like Blondin,
over the Niagara of oblivion.
His best-loved work is a pastorale,
composed behind closed shutters
to block out the mugissements
of the marching Prussians, the cries
of the Communards up against the walls
of the Père Lachaise. The people who praised

his stubborn devotion to his art
have gone to their graves or chosen
silence. "La petite phrase de Vinteuil"
a fictional composer invented
by his younger and socially invisible
contemporary, Marcel Quelconque,
is unhummable but better known.

What is easiest forgotten
is why any of this might be remembered,
less lasting than bronze plaques
or original scores preserved under glass.
With Empyrean calm, the composer
sits comfortably now with his own minority.
His modest ranking on the zeitgeist index
means nothing in eternity. He watches
the mortals left behind, clinging to drifting
data like shipwrecked sailors, within their grasp
all of History and none of it.

Panguna

Leavings from a mine on Bougainville,
a pool of slurry with a rainbow tinge on top
transmogrified into Art Doco at the Gallery.
The face of the local woman sifting and stirring
has the depth and texture of a map of sorrow.
The mine was a pot of gold to offshore stakeholders
till it went belly up, the jobs jobs jobs they promised,
nothing but a dirty trickle of royalties, then a past
and future that had lost all meaning. Thousands
of dead in the name of budget repair to the opaque
personal accounts of kleptocrats and the pale
myth of the sturdy integrity of a nation-state.
We could learn from this but haven't and won't,
about land loyally tenanted but never owned.

Navigation

A blind woman is being taught to use a cane
by a carer taught to conjure up total darkness
and translate it into imagined geometry.

She's newly blind perhaps through illness or mishap
or having crossed a line from partial sight
to the status of object, mere displacement of air.

Is the street completely unfamiliar or newly so,
turned into a slalom course of jostle and shinbark,
or a field of unknown depth that needs sounding?

For a sighted person, it is like trying to remember
a child's unnameable world of unknowing.
You can shut your eyes in a parody of empathy

knowing you can open them on what was there before
and feel ashamed of taking for granted
a fragile, fallible thing, so easily tricked

by a magician's patter and business. You look
at the buildings opposite, a forest of shapes:
torches, wafer-biscuits, giant cell-phones,

all standing on end, with a gap in the middle,
half-obscured, that has to be guessed at:
a crater hollowed out by a meteorite, more

predictably, an excavation for underground
parking, a grassed space, a squat old building
saved and cocooned in new surroundings.

You have a context to guess from. For the blind,
the visual context is zero, data from the other
senses, but otherwise, all gap and conjecture.

Out of the corner of your eye that is spreading,
your optometrist warns, slowly and inexorably
towards the other corner, are the blurred shapes

of the carer and the blind woman who have edged
their way to a point between you and your bus-stop.
You skirt around them, aiming a nod and a smile

at the carer, then, inexplicably, at the blind woman,
as if a smile could send vibrations through the air,
perceptible to a sixth sense called in to replace

the one lost, or perhaps just a wasted gesture
of fellow-feeling, drifting off into the dark
for the pure relief and pleasure of the giver.

Recent Poems 2019 –

Z-O-M-B-I-E

Unquick, undead, with oyster eyes, he surfs
a toppled tombstone then lurches and trundles

through the poplars, unshapes himself like
an octopus to shimmy through the iron grille

of the perimeter then negotiates a rope-bridge
between definitions: of being and non-being,

immanence and evanescence, the engendered
and the cobbled-together, a zonked mis-stepping

bi-pedal, his flipped orbs miming introspection,
his ragged dentition snapping at shadows.

If he hadn't been wiped clean of awareness
like a knife, to make him a mere instrument

of the dark forces, to prowl the mean streets of
eschatology, he would know he was doomed

and could stride from his shelter into an unpeopled
waste, like Captain Oates taking one for the team.

But a poignant scenario belongs in another studio.
In this one he's a pop-up transplant clinic

harvesting useful parts for the highest bidders
with scraps for himself to keep him ticking over.

His to serve out the term of his dead cat bounce
for those near-dead masters who consume the living.

A Sentence from Adrian McKinty

Dublin to London through a pall of cloud and
glimpses of grey sea with white corrugations.
A sentence rises from the crime novel on my lap
and stakes its claim to the rest of the story:

"Her words were frozen birds fallen from the telegraph wires"

in the slanting rain over the littered streets and gutted houses
of Belfast in 1980, season of departures and separations.
But the "Dear John" message is of every time and place
and every medium, from smoke-trail to voice-mail:
"Is there someone else?" "Why wouldn't there be?"
"You're the right person at the wrong time and place" or some
permutation of the same elements. "We can still see each other
after the Spring Term" but we both know we won't.

It's all over bar the shouting and there won't, thank God,
be any of that. We were always better than that together
and will stay that way to remember who we were
for each other, who we can be again for someone else
and the children we will have with someone else.

And my heart lets go like a frozen bird.

Not Me Too

Hollywood has changed but not much. Howard
Hughes in his roll-in-the-hay-day was worse.
Hard headed girls might have put out with a shrug,
but others were still shuddering ten years later.
These were the ones the cruel sleaze liked best.
In the saddest cases, child brides were sold out
twice: by family then the husband who tried to
shake Hughes down for the price of a quick divorce.

I wasn't taken in. I saw this one coming,
so to speak, no need to be a mind-reader.
It helps at the audition if you turn up with a
lawyer and a Sumo wrestler. So I said, "Harvey,
what say YOU wear a suit that fits if you can
find one and I wear the bathrobe and give you
a quick flash, can you make do with that?"
He was the best thing that never happened to
my career, and I to his. Pity I didn't go in harder
for the sake of my unluckier sisters who
had more to lose. As for the Walmart girls
with a creepy manager, what about them?

A Party at the Retirement Village

for the 90th birthday of a veteran of a left-wing
theatre group who knows where the bodies are buried
and the costumes they wore. She is introduced by
her ASIO file number and some of her old friends
recite their own numbers in plainsong like an audition
for bingo-callers. The guest of honour reads a passage
from her file as if she is dancing a waltz with her
shadow-self though it isn't clear who is leading
and who following: "I know who started that rumour,"
she says. "It was me, but the silly bastard passed it on
and gave himself away. Gotcha! Thirty percent of the
members were ASIO. One I recall was a great dancer,
good-looking too. He must have been the honey-trap."

A sketch is performed in the style of the topical
revues of the theatre's early days, a cross between
agitprop and music-hall. The whole knees-up
(easier said than done these days) is a bit theatrical
and why on earth not? We've still got our chops!

A blue-rinsed lady hovers in the wings,
a resident, I think, but a self-appointed
keeper of order who is making sure
the Communists don't steal the silver.

Change of life

(a meditation on "Aurore" a film by Blandine Lenoir)

"Aurore", rosy dawn, a name that flashes a signal
to social historians: "born 68 or thereabouts"
a name that trails a heritage of poetic diction
after it as the years pass and an invitation
to irony as hopes sag and the body lets you down
as it always must, in hot flushes and treacherous
chemistry. The streets of your town have grown
moody too in their fashion, shoulders that bump
their way to somewhere else, eyes that look past you.
A middle-aged man behind you whispers: "Nice arse"
which it still is, but when you round on him, he turns
to stone. The you, which still feels like you, wears
the face of the Medusa. It's not so long surely since
young men called you "stunning" and they weren't
lying. After sex, they often looked stunned.

Your new boss at the restaurant plants you
behind the counter to put your best torso forward
in dim light. He renames you and casts you
as "Queen Bee", somewhere between a Grandma
and a brothel Madame for your sexy protégées.
You tell him to get stuffed in the nicest possible way
in terms of your own satisfaction.

At the job-placement office, a bloke tries to coach you
on interview techniques, the sort of bloke who sees
menstruation as temporary insanity and the menopause
as a long dark night of the soul for the woman and
everyone else around her. "A cruel demographic"
he explains. His or yours? He's a near-contemporary
and a self-important "con" (in French not a "scammer"

but a hopeless dickhead) and you tell him so. You
won't be treated as a fool by someone you probably
helped with his homework at High School.

"Between jobs" you work as a volunteer companion
and helper in a sort of share-house and co-op for
a cohort of forthright and independent older women,
eloquent, well-educated feminists of a bygone age.
They defer to Hortense, a leader by seniority and rude health.
She tells you a tale of passionate trysts with a lover
now "separated by life". She describes the final
climax (not a tautology) that sounds like a passage
from an elegant pornographic novel by Apollinaire.
You ask "When did all this happen?"
"Three years ago" she says.

Le Retour d'Age (Change of Life), the turning-point
of a woman's life when it all starts to go downhill?
or a cup half-full: "still life in the old girl yet" or something
with more dignity and strength, in a tone that men,
(curse them and bless them...a cup half-full)
struggle to find even in an empty room.

The Endless Story

A woman at the bus-stop, mid-twenties,
face resting in a neutral zone, hers or mine.
She turns, showing the words on the back of her
tee-shirt: "MY EX DIED" in block capitals,
off-centre and smeared so it looks home-made,
though probably stamped in a factory somewhere
in Asia. So why would I think the message
is for me? Since I'm the only one not fiddling
with a phone? Is that more self-centred or less?

A message on a shirt should be something you own
that can start a conversation or have the last word.
This is an enigma through its lack of context,
expansion or affective potential, like an offcut
from a random sample of internet traffic. Was the Ex
a violent loser, a strangler-vine around her life?
Is this what she wants to share? Not likely. Too young
to have had a long struggle, threats or custody battles,
a history that would show in her eyes. She doesn't match,
pecking away at her phone like everyone else.

So let's suppose the Ex was a casual flatmate,
promoted to friend then friend with benefits,
boyfriend, then slipping back in the ranks
to companion second-class, notable mostly
for his always-thereness. Did he leave a letter
suggesting still waters running deeper than she knew?
Is she telling us she's hurting, wants us to know,
not just connecting to some vague sorority of grief.

The woman starts to disappear into her function.
She's a courier only, bearing a sealed report from
nowhere to no fixed address. It's the message itself

I feel sorry about, its tale docked, a castaway on a
boat full of rootless stories, bobbing in the shifting
channels of a sea of uncaring, that needs the tragic
dimension it was reaching for, a sense of resolution.

If the woman were from a war-zone, the Ex a lone
survivor of a cohort of friends she grew up with…
How could I go there? I can't even watch the News,
the endless sweep of the suffering, a slow dulling
of responses prompting a shame that flares
then flutters and droops like a blown rose.

I'm pinning donkeys on tails that were meant
to be what they are. Afflatus interruptus, best left
to its own devices. Look at the faces around you.
Eye contact means cuts and abrasions. Get a life,
old man. Make a Blog of yourself. Pour out your heart.

At the Azalea Motel

the standard double is a spare sort of dainty
fitted and furnished in déjà vu like a
crime-scene cleaned to the status quo ante
except for its aura. You feel you should try
to impose the ghost of an invasive
narrative, shortsheet the bed, cut
a deep triple-six into the pages
of the Bible, sit a plush-toy spider monkey
at the desk in the corner, fix a sign
in wedding-invitation font to the bedhead:
"This is not at all what it looks like.
We are travelling companions and just friends."

From the bench in the back garden
I hear a branch spring up softly
with a sound like a silk camisole
dropped onto tissue-paper
and watch a King Parrot take to the air.
A leaf falls in a stuttering
trajectory, crisp and jagged
as the roof of a pagoda.
Is this the leaf which triggers the
cyclone that flattens San Diego?

From frogspawn to Prince.
Upward to lightness on extended
wings. What is the sound
of one lip smacking? What
can a tap of God's hammer mean
with no one to witness it?

There's a path further on into a patch of forest,
like the motel site and the fields behind, part

of my grandfather's farm long ago. An old
mine-shaft filled in and boarded over. A faint
rock-carving now under fresh-sprayed graffiti.
Beyond, even the topography seems insecure,
a creek gone missing, hills with tops lopped off,
gullies plumped up with tailings and landfill.

Memory plays the tricks we teach it. We are deaf
and blind to objective measures. Distances are
spanned in our minds at the walking pace of a
five-year-old. Our sense of neighbourhood is lapped
by the pace of change, rests in pools of reminiscence
like chains of billabongs when the river shifts course.
What can we do but take it personally,
a sly identity theft while we are sleeping.

An exercise in the Lydian Mode of Lexical Improvisation

tatterdemalion: A person in ragged clothes (origin unknown)

Not so.

Le Vicomte Tata de Malion, an eighteenth century Gascon noble, had dissipated the family fortune in taverns and gambling-dens. He was a man of epicene mien and eccentric attire who bet such reckless amounts that a hush settled over the gaming-tables whenever he appeared, a hush where you could hear a pin drop or the heavy breathing of moths and silverfish as they turned his trailing frock-coat into streamers.

His name surfaced in later centuries in the limerick contests of British universities, mostly as a challenge to rhymesters. "Pygmalion" and "epithalamion" were popular solutions but desperate concoctions like "take Arthur Waley on" "put Trevor Bailey on" or "Battersea alien" generally earned a fine and suspension from the High Table.

As standards slipped over the decades, the Vicomte was replaced as a yardstick for rhymesters by the likes of Diana Dors (born Diana Fluck), a British actress of the 1950's. In more recent times, names like Thatcher and Berlusconi have come into their own, without, as yet, making a permanent contribution to the language.

Fantoma

Norman Tompkins, a senior tutor at a Midlands University and respected regional poet, leapt to a qualified prominence in Academic circles by translating extracts from a selection of minor but unjustly neglected Hungarian poets, among them Laszlo Kiss, the Young Werther of Warszowa, who lamented his exile and his inability to love generously in a series of starkly depressive sonnets. Another standout was Roland Rado, bard of a revolutionary cell in Timisoara at the turn of the last century whose percussive texts still resonate. So also for Attila Karolyi, the footloose flâneur, equally at home in Vienna or Sarajevo, casual chronicler of the last agonies of Empire. Jan Gabor, who died at 21 in an equestrian accident, left behind a single slim manuscript found decades later in the personal effects of a former governess.

It was generally agreed that the translations broke new ground, eclipsing all earlier efforts which are all but forgotten and deservedly out of print. It was only when the Hungarian Embassy thanked him for his cross-cultural labours and proposed a cash grant and Residency with the Writers Collective of Szolnok that Norman realised that he had a problem. The original manuscripts were elusive as indeed were the biographies of the poets. In short, he had made it all up.

"I didn't mean for it to go this far" said Norman. "I'm not even much of a linguist, really. I used to do these impressions of Morel père from the pages of 'Sons and Lovers' in Nottingham dialect—went over a treat at the local readings. Then, I suppose, I got a bit too clever..."

An Unofficial Source at the Palace

Harry is letting the side down.
The Royals are not as ordinary men.
Some of them are women, God bless them.
Others are not too sure and some have been
out-and-out woopsies but this was kept
under wraps and it still is, though it didn't
matter and still doesn't, provided you cut
the ribbon and shut up or even say something
daft or wet so long as you don't sound like
someone who plays darts in the pub. And
the Royals have power, not the off-with-his-head
kind but they have an army, a team of spies
and bullies and a gaggle of media lickspittles
who'll give you a good trolling if you go
republican or any other kind of bolshie.
You have to be heroic
croupier-faced and stoic.
Sorry for the couplet. I used to be a bit of a luvvie
before I got a tap on the shoulder: Duke
of Cork and Leather. A Royal equerry,
chooser of saddles and sherry.

You have to take one for the team,
suffer fools and rogues not gladly
but in a manner stately and impassive.
You can't even roll your eyes gently
or lift an eyebrow, like Angele Merkel
in the presence of Trump. It works a treat
in pantomime but with the whole world watching!
Nice enough woman in some ways but a bit
common. So off you go, Harry. Play darts
with your mates but keep your eye on the Arab
chappie at the billiard-table, with a bulge in his pants

and holding a cue by the skinny end. He's pleased
to see you, in the worst possible way.

If the Daily Mail's paying
I might saddle up for another.
Triple Royal Bristol Special Reserve.
You wrote it down.

A Memo from the Dean

"Re the question you set for the First Semester Assignment.
At first glance it seems generously open-ended —
'Write something interesting about market research'
but the tone is imperious, not to say paternalistic,
and in view of the skewing in the gender
distribution of your class, provocative,
not the quality we expect in a seasoned Academic.
The bias in favour of native English-speakers
(non fee-paying some of them) is embarrassingly obvious.
One might be tempted to think that the cancellation
of your course on the Metaphysical Poets and your necessary
re-assignment have occasioned a fit of pique.
For the moment, consider yourself counselled (Strike One).
Strike Two is mandatory re-enrolment in the course:
'Seven Types of Accountability' at the School of Management.
Six months successful probation and we wipe the slate clean.
Yours in Collegiate Responsibility,

The Dean

Abstinence

A social cricket match in the 1960's:
Surfing International versus the Paddington Push.
The Push opener calls for a quick single:
"Will we, Rodney, will we?" "Yes, by God, we will!"
The surfer stands upright and balances
before he throws and they get home easily.

Sub-cultures at the time didn't shun the mainstream.
Libertarian punters made whimsical all-up bets.
Abstract painters drank and played darts all night
in a wharfies' pub near the Quay. And the mainstream
took them pretty much as they found them: harmless
nutters mostly, good for a laugh. No bullshit posing
on either side and it was all OK. Identity politics with
an adversarial edge? Abstain! Another schooner?

They were all larger than life as the night wore on,
Colourful Identities but of a benign and operable kind.
Were there ladies in the house? A few, more than there
used to be, a bit robust and feisty, quips and whips at
twenty paces but their smiles were infectious. Some
were the first generation of their families to go to Uni,
as much their fathers' daughters as their mothers', who
knew the language and ethos of the places they were in.

Suburbs were slower to change then and most of them
liked it that way. Social transformation was too much fun
to rush the process. Nostalgia? We all know not to trust it.
We're talking about a few inner-city pubs that were far
from family friendly. It wasn't much but it was a start.

Portals

into a world of masks and noms de nerd
no labels and faux labels
sputtering interior monologues
turned inside-out so they show
themselves to the world while life as such
is subterranean sub-venusian,
subliminal. The text untampered
stumbles on while the punctuation
in the form of food and drink
drugs and troubled sleep
flickers somewhere behind the eyes.
No context, no plot, no character
development beyond an endless
adolescence where possibilities
stiffen and freeze. There seems
to be no way out of the cave
with its myriad glow worm
twinkles, the chorus of happy-
clappy roaming synapses.
My school reference said
I was self-possessed, as if the self
kept itself to itself and couldn't
be pinned and shredded
couldn't be beside itself
insisting that this is only research
which it was at the start
till half of me was watching
the other half lost and losing
the will to save itself like a
diver suffering from rapture
of the deep and wondering
how hard could it be
to click a damn

mouse.

I allowed myself six weeks to research a story on chat rooms and took
twice as long.
It was dreary at times but had a peculiar fascination that risked
becoming addictive.
Unlike the gonzo journalists of another era, who infiltrated Hells
Angels and neo-nazi
groups, I ran no physical risk but at the end I felt exhausted and
diminished in some existential way. Like the gonzo journalists, I have
made the story of my own research
part of the larger story.

Angst

Antennae saluting
hackles on the up and up
a dog-whistle bellied out like a siren
because I forgot to take the pills I forgot to collect
after I forgot to be tested and get a prescription.
My condition is self-generating
self-sustaining and obviously
self-conscious. Each nervous tic
has a nervous tic and all are listed
by the ATO as dependents.
We are a closely-settled colony here
that looks for Lebensraum in all directions
so lock up your daughters, sons and pets
and the deeds to your house.
Put the lot under Second Amendment protection.
It's a family thing. The hand of my uncle
is fixing a lock on the pen of my aunt.
In the yard, my Doberman
is burying the arm of my
parole-officer.

The Glow Worm Cave

Twelve souls on a barque in a river of the Underworld
seek the light scattered in tiny emerald clusters, each
coalescing into a pinprick of luminescence. The boat
swings in circles, thudding into the rock walls.
The rushing of the waters is a kind of plainsong,
a metronomic pulsing that forces us inwards into our
own thoughts. We are told to still our tongues. On exit
we bow our heads and count slowly to seven. There are
two services daily in the shrine of St. Lampyris at Te Anau
with a young priestess as keeper of the torch
of deliverance and the opacity of secrets.

Back in the well-lit warmth of the little theatre,
we pilgrims are treated to a short film
on the life of the glow worm, how she sets
her "fishing-lines" of sticky thread to trap
the moths she feeds on, slowly sucking
the life out of them to give her strength
for a flurry of mating to take the breath away.
It is a tale of ambush, cruelty, murder,
territorial wars and matter-of-fact cannibalism.

The left brain files the facts for easy retrieval
while the right brain takes me back to the cave
to keep my Eleusinian Mysteries mysterious,
points of orientation at a vigil in the dark places,
a web of fitful stars in a sea of unknowing.

A Review

An old friend, a talented lady
who has lived like many
in the shadow of others,
has produced, after a long gestation,
a novel which I'm pleased to see reviewed
till I read the review, which is,
in a word, bad. I want
to ring her to tell her
I wish   I wish
the review had been better —
than she deserves? No. —
than it was. I wish...
and am tempted here to hang
a calumny around the neck of the reviewer
which would be unworthy of me
and by implication, of her,
my friend that is. I wish...
she had shown the draft to me first —
and not to her agent? Or her husband? No. —
I wish...   her well.
As always. I wish
her well and want
to give every breath of softness
to the phrase and every ounce
of gravity. I wish...
it had been otherwise.

Sonny at Seventy-Seven

(Sonny Rollins at the Sydney Opera House 1-6-08)

He says in an interview: "Every day
brings something new physically." Not bad.
Not even unsettling. Just new.
The hair and beard are white, he walks
with a shuffle and his wave is cheerful
but a little sketchy, as if to say:
"Waving is OK but it's not what I do."
What he does is what he has done
for sixty years, the big generous tone,
the flurry of notes so fast it gives
an aural illusion of massed chords.
If anything was lost over the years,
it was replaced by something just as difficult,
or more so, as if the virtuosity
would sicken and die if forced to pace
around the bounds of the same enclosure.
After a two-hour set and a long encore,
the djinni is finally back in the bottle
and he makes his way to the wings a little
gingerly. This is the happiest of men.

Last Known Address

A message board with his own name, the date
of his next birthday, the age he will be and names
of family members past and present that cover
four generations, old photos of himself at various
ages, in various roles, on and off stage, the last
of himself on a tennis-court, aged 73, and probably
smashing a winner to close the set. They are like
cue-cards to remind him who he was and still
notionally is. There are greetings in two foreign
languages he still speaks fluently if kick-started
by a patient visitor, rare these days, since those
best qualified are dead, no longer fluent or even
ambulant.

    The carer who has been working his wing
for the last week wears a large name tag and her
nation of origin, Nepal, so he won't have to keep
asking and telling her "you're the pretty one"
since she knows already and might prefer: "you're
the nice one" or "you're the one who knows what
she's doing" which might be unfair to some of her
colleagues but not all of them.

    He's reading a newspaper aloud like the
actor he used to be getting the feel of a new script
but he would need a synopsis of page one of two
in a skeletal "breaking news" piece of about 500
words. He knows my face at once and knows that
I speak his language, fluent English of another
time and place, but I need ID, CV and short bio
to put myself in full focus.

    I haven't been back since the virus forced
limits on visitors, but as I left last time, it struck me
that if somewhere like this was my Last Stop,
it wouldn't take long to pack, no time at all. If I still

had it together enough to do my own packing, there'd be no need to go. A journey to the end of the night is something I wouldn't go gently into.

On a Suspect Ancestry Web Site

News of my great-great-grandfather at last. Eureka!
(one of the few disasters, it seems, that he wasn't
present at). He was a man of bumbling origins
who aspired to mediocrity, achieved it early,
clung to it and hung on grimly to the last.
He was survived by a brood of sullen heirs
who didn't fall far from the tree and some of them
were lucky not to swing from one. I might have better
luck with my great-great-grandmother. The women
in my family were always smarter than the dimwits
who deserted them, a trend that might have started
back in the mists of time measured by Grandfather
Clock and bundy. "A wardrobe-mistress of Lola
Montez" and there's more...! An ancestor-person
an old luvvie like me can be proud of! Unwittingly,
she made me the man I am today! I might try a click
on a dodgy web site called "Medium".

Memorial Grove

Near the Writers Centre
on the grounds of the old asylum
is an avenue of trees stripped and lopped
into grim fairytale shapes, mutilations
and sinister silhouettes. The torsos
look stout enough but I'm not a tree-doctor
so they might have been punished
for reasons of health and safety.
I'm hoping it's not a stealthy prelude
to total removal of the diseased
lungs of the city for the general good
of developers and sinking funds.

There's a town in Tasmania where a
stricken War Memorial grove was groomed
by a sculptor into timber statues
of soldiers, ambulances and horses
from the armies of the Great War.
They could set such a man to work
on the ex-greenery of the grounds
to produce a gallery of famous lunatics
from the not-such-glory days, for example
the Archibald of the Archibald Art Prize,
Bea Miles lurching from a battered taxi...
I hope there's a tree the measure of my uncle,
who was built like a tree, it seemed to me as a child,
but whose seasonal changes were swifter and sharper.
He walked the grounds for forty years, talking
to the trees, to absent friends and especially
enemies, whoever and whatever couldn't talk back.

He refused release into the community, claiming
that this was for his own and his country's good.

He thought himself a better judge of his status
than the health bureaucrats who wanted
to clear the books and the premises
for reasons quite other than the welfare
of patients or potential victims of their own
bad decisions. I imagine a sculpture
of a wooden-faced Uncle John rampant
over the heavy roller with deadly intent,
administering strict discipline to the cricket pitch,
spitting venom at the revolting turf and muttering:
"That will teach you to mind your own business"

Inheritance

My family tree tells me that I am one-eighth Jewish.
What might this mean? An old comrade from University
said recently that I was the first Catholic friend he ever had.
"You're kidding! We were both agnostics!" "But you were
a Catholic agnostic" meaning whatever he chose it to mean.
Making small talk, I once told a teacher of Hebrew of my
Jewish connection. "In the maternal line?" she said,
"You could marry a nice Jewish girl." "My wife,"
I said, "wouldn't like that". "Is she anti-semitic?"
Was one of us joking, neither or both?

I claim no kinship with Einstein, Freud or Georges Perec;
"Quod scripsi, scripsi. Quod fui, fui." The language
of the victors of Masada but I have been tempted to
identify with people who got under the skin of the Emperors
and Dictators who called them: "rootless cosmopolitans",
people for whom property was precarious and were forced
to keep their assets between their ears or hidden in cavities,
people of a slippery definition as a means of self-defence.
Twelve and a half percent? Impressive as an interest rate
but in terms of conferring responsibility or the right
to tell Jewish jokes, zero. "A parrot walked into a bar
in the Bronx with a rabbi on his shoulder..." et cetera.
A Jewish comedian might get away with it but not me.

My great-great-grandparents were listed on the ship's register
as "Jewish". His occupation was given as "Mining Engineer"
and they went to Portland, not far from where the first gold strikes
were made a few years earlier. There wouldn't have been a Jewish
community or synagogue in Portland. Perhaps they were already
agnostic in their hearts and paid lip-service only to the notion
of being Jewish. They were certainly never "converts". Closer
to the present, the family were comfortable with their status

as non-churchgoers. Like many American secular Jews, they supported trade unionism and human rights, the part of the story that I claim as my inheritance. The spiritual part of the history? My last surviving uncle survived Changi, had been a champion walker and stalwart of the University Athletics Club, a man of endurance and strong character. If he had Supernatural help with this, he never said so. If someone else had inferred this, he would have listened to them with the greatest respect.

Projection

There's a ghost tour of the reef by styrofoam Esky.
Our energy needs are met by a symbiotic harnessing
of flood, tempest, anger and Acts of God.
The homeless nest in barrios of luxury yachts
and jetsam blown ashore on slag-pile hillsides.
There's peace of a kind in the micro-dynamics
of island villages: gated estates and predators
facing off in an adversarial balance of terror.

A crow with a hoard of golf balls, eyeballs and shredded plastic
for his mate and the fat, pale channel-bill cuckoo chick
that has pushed the eggs and crowlets out of the nest.
It's a metaphor for where and how we live.

We all message in a hundred characters max
then an interrobang thus: (?!) to show vehemence
feeding on ignorance, release on sardonic excess
for a flurry of cyber-cuddles and high-fives.
Gin-slings on the patio under bleary stars,
gentle goodnights and last hurrahs.

Dropping Off at the Work Station

I am paddling in the shallows of sleep
where dreams spawn in the weed-beds.
The voices are having their way with me again:
the Inspector wants me to sign something

and issues a caution: "Don't read it.
It will only upset you." A hedge-fund manager
in a suit made from porcupine-pelts
delivers a rodomontade: "I earned every cent

because I took the trouble to read the entrails."
The next voice is mine but issuing
from another face I can't quite identify:
"Doctor, Doctor, there are people out there

who mean to hurt me." "Of course,"
says the quack, "I know most of them.
I'll write you a prescription for a handgun."
The computer is playing headmaster again:

"I have it on excellent information
that you have performed an illegal operation.
Press any key and you are in even deeper trouble.
This could mean the loss of your scholarship."

A classroom full of spoilt children
texting. I tell the Protection Unit:
"Asking them to listen is not verbal abuse.
Verbal abuse goes like this: are you ready...?"

The Human Resources person asks me to name
three things I most like about the workplace.
No, not the long unpaid lay-off at Christmas.
And don't ask "three?" with a silly look on your face.

The bloke from "Ancestry" gives it to me straight:
"Family folklore is a dodgy starting-point.
Your forebears were indeed convicts and rightly so.
How can I put this? 'Unspeakably vile' comes to mind."

A dozen new voices that sound like leaf-blowers
are warming up in the green room for the next
performance of "The Suburbs of Purgatory".
Will no one rid me of this turbulent circuitry?

Drones

*"I took a week to learn to fly the Panvic Mini-drone
then I felt like a pro. You'll love it to bits."*— *(first-time droner)*

The pictures they can't show on the News
are seen by the drone-pilots sitting in trailers
in Nevada, who can have bad dreams without
leaving their own backyards: blood spatters
steaming like spills from a stock-pot, body parts
scraped off walls with a trowel, collateral damage
in the shape of children appearing from nowhere.

The strikes depend on intelligence on the ground.
There are mistakes in good faith: if they were sure
of their ground, they wouldn't need drones, though
they would take more losses. Mistakes in bad faith too:
high-value-targets and drug-dealers fingering their
rivals to take them off the board; ambitious Generals,
even the President, calling strikes for personal gain
and lying about outcomes or motives with complete
impunity, in the name of National Security. Could you
use a drone to spread a deadly virus among your enemies?
Possible but tricky. As with mustard gas in the Great War,
when the wind might change and blow it all back on you.

Public-Private partnership in weapons systems
is ideologically sacred and no longer challenged.
It opens doors to profiteers and privateers, gives
spies and hackers new and softer targets. No genie
ever goes back in the bottle but this one
takes its wares on the road in double-time.
To make big money, you have to think big,
like Apple or Google where the sky's the limit:
Mom-'n- Pop drones from Amazon delivered by drone;

courier-drones that don't sweat or shout or want
paid holidays, Super or Health Insurance;
self-defence drones, Second Amendment drones;
Drone Fairs, Drone-a-thons, frequent flyer points;
dronelets that fit in holsters or shopping-bags;
offshore drones flying to the Cayman Islands.

Drones for recreational use, like drugs,
might not be harmless. Overfly an airfield, the home
of your daughter's cocaine dealer, or your ex-wife
in flagrante in the pool with her lawyer. You may
get some flak or at least an Avionics Veto Order.
A Drone Club for the blokes from the Men's Shed
or their sons and grandsons with an electronics habit
may need a planning permit with strict conditions
that reek of Big Government and incite to riot.

What a lot of weight to bear for what started off
as a fragile beautiful thing that could soar like a poem,
mimic the flight-pattern of a frigatebird, the silhouette
of a partridge, wheel in concert with a squadron of
swallows, be insidious and deadly like a snake which is
also beautiful. Poems too can be pure in their intentions
or at least mute, as good as the people who make them
or use them but for good or ill, they make nothing happen.

Twilight

The addiction shelves in fridge or cabinet.
The "who-was-that-in-the-old-photo" room.
Yellowed pages unturned for fifty years.
The nostalgia head-space   the aftertaste
of a nightmare   spaces
where good intentions past and present
go to die

set against your living reality
your growth in a soft frame
of continuity   a space
where breathing will make sense
to the last   a void
to come to terms with
a time when contours melt
and the stars do what they must

Acknowledgements

Poems in this book have appeared in the following:

The Poetry Magazine, New Poetry, Poetry Australia, Newcastle Prize Anthologies 1999 and 2000, Blue Dog, Small Packages, Harbour City Poems (Puncher & Wattmann), Canberra Times, Island, Best Australian Poetry, Best Australian Poems, Meanjin, Quadrant, Southerly, Famous Reporter, Wet Ink, Australian Poetry Journal, Antipodes, Spineless Wonders Anthologies, Contemporary Australian Poetry (Puncher & Wattmann), *Cordite, Canberra VC Prize Anthologies 2014, 2015, 2017, 4W, Poetry d'Amour Anthology 2020*